W9-DJI-691

Authentic
GUITAR-TAB
Edition ™
Includes Complete Solos

James Taylor: GREATEST HITS

Something in the way she moves
Carolina in my mind
Fire and rain
Sweet Baby James
Country road
You've got a friend
Don't let me be lonely tonight
Walking man
How sweet it is
Mexico
Shower the people
Steamroller

CONTENTS

Key To Notation Symbols

Something in the way she moves

Words and Music by
JAMES TAYLOR

*Capo at 3rd fret. The number 3 in tab represents a capoed open string.

that seems— to leave— this trou - bled world be- hind.

Substitute Fill 1 on D.S.

If I'm feel-in' down. an' blue—

or trou - bled by—— some fool- ish game,— she al -

Fill 1

*Fast volume swells

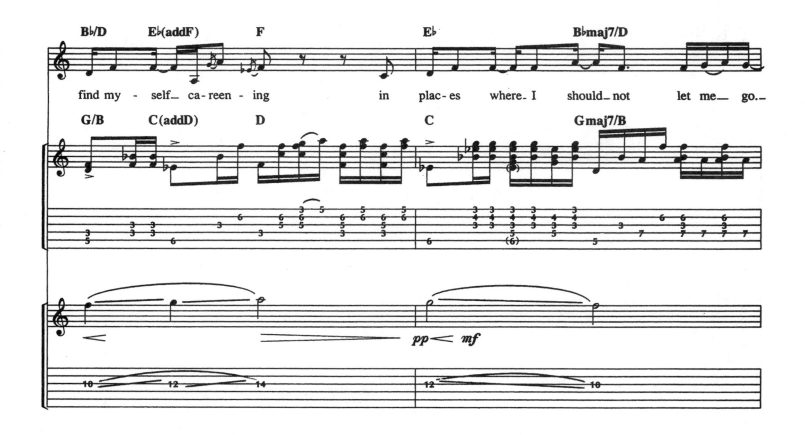

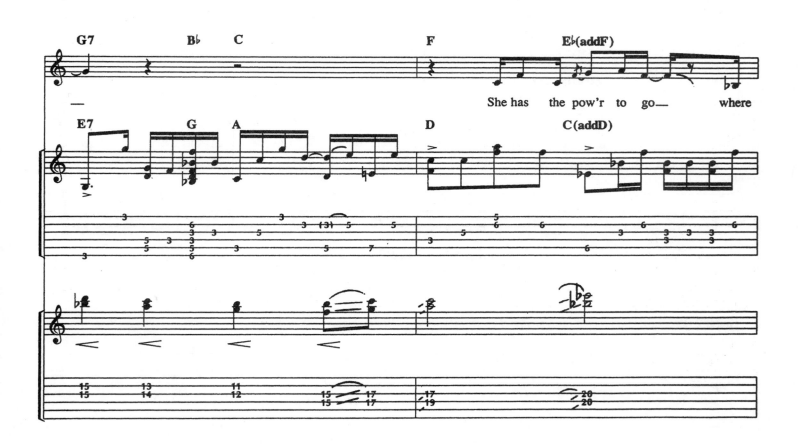

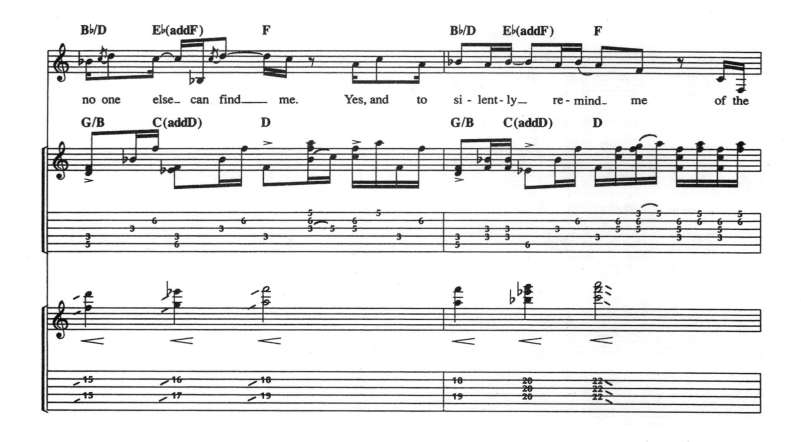

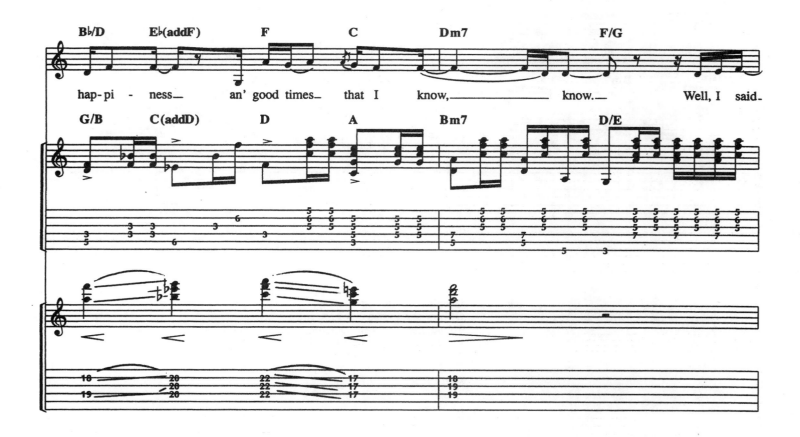

Additional Lyrics

Verse 2:   It isn't what she's got to say,
Or how she thinks or where she's been.
To me, the words are nice the way they sound.
I like to hear them best that way.
It doesn't much matter what they mean,
Well, she says them mostly just to calm me down.
And I feel . . .

Carolina in my mind

Words and Music by
JAMES TAYLOR

In my mind I'm gone to Car-o-li-na.

Can't you see the sun-shine? Can't you just feel the moon shin-ing?

*Capo at 2nd fret.

14

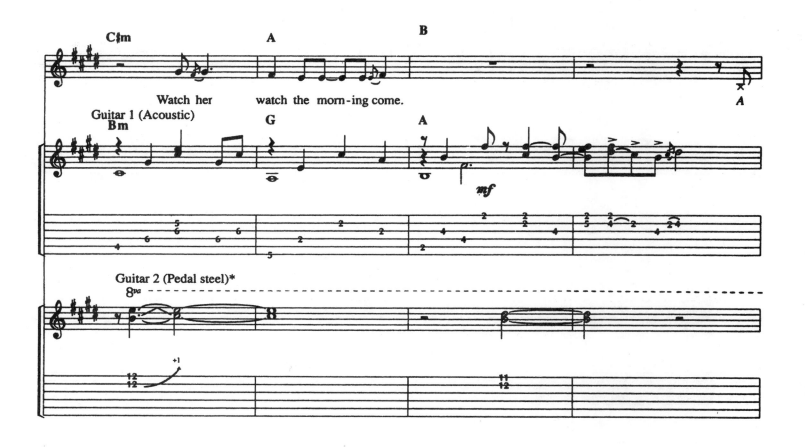

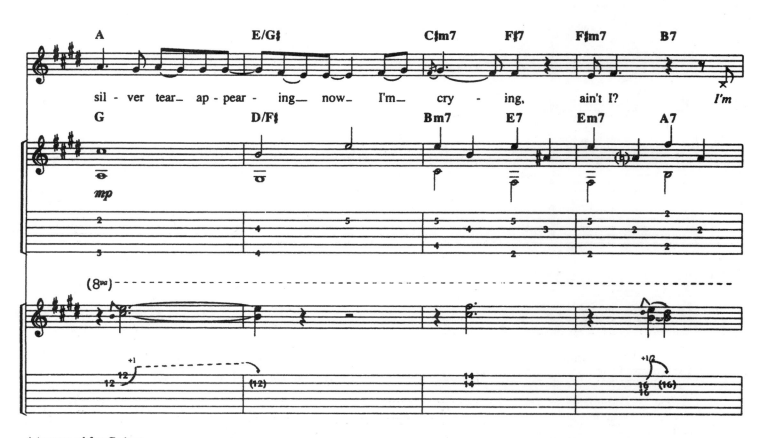

*Arranged for Guitar

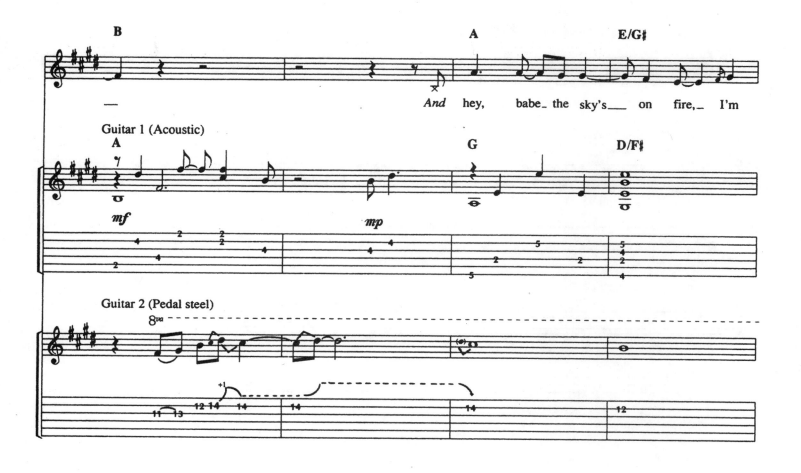

And hey, babe_ the sky's__ on fire,__ I'm

Guitar 1 (Acoustic)

Guitar 2 (Pedal steel)

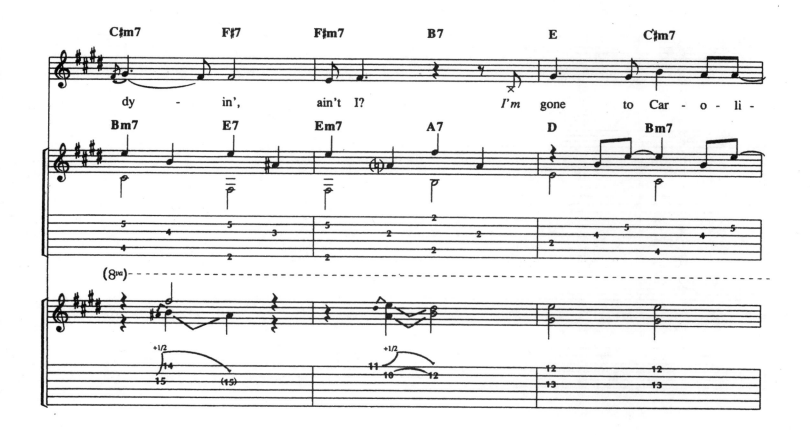

dy - in', ain't I? I'm gone to Car - o - li -

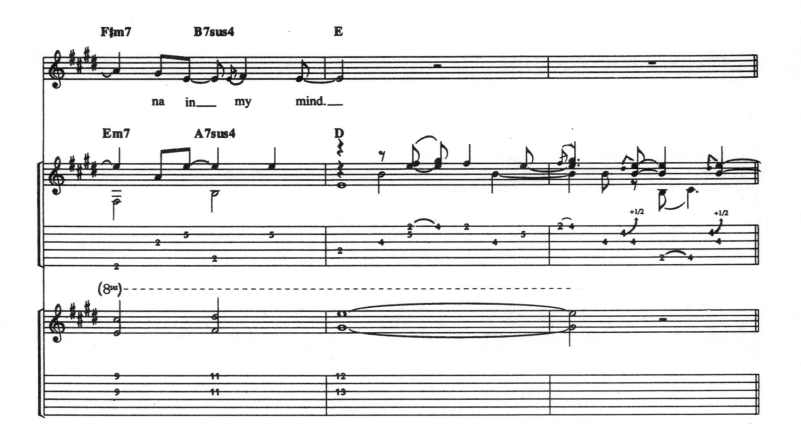

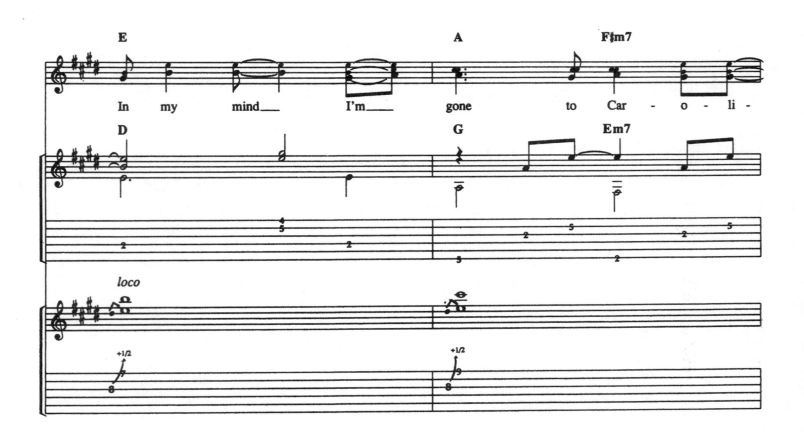

na.

A

Can't you see the sun -

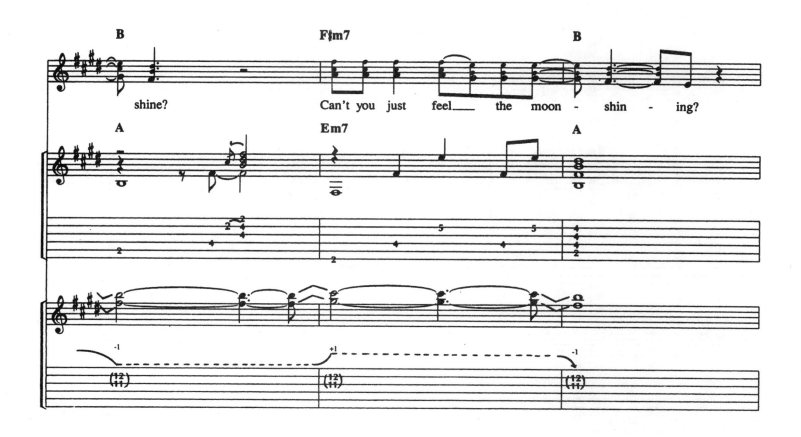

B

shine?

F♯m7

Can't you just feel___ the moon - shin - ing?

B

A

Em7

A

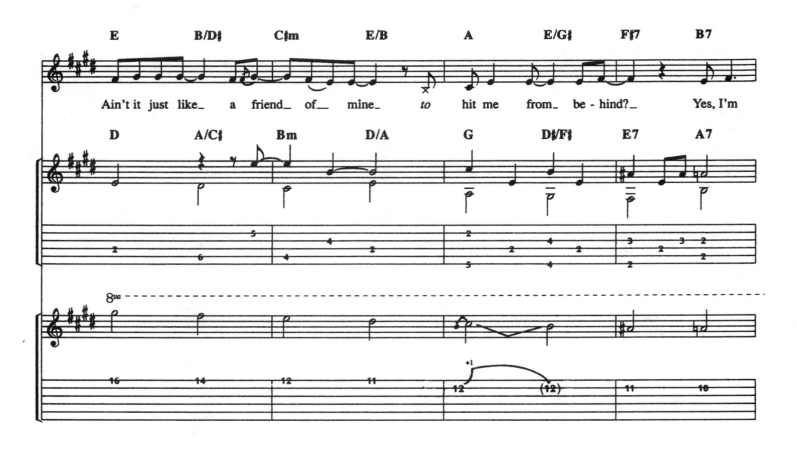

Ain't it just like_ a friend_ of_ mine_ *to* hit me from_ be - hind?_ Yes, I'm

gone to Car - o - li - na in_ my mind._

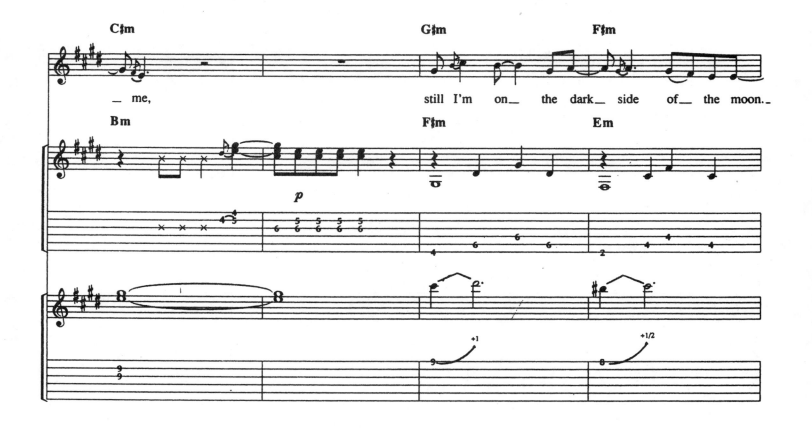

_ me, still I'm on_ the dark_ side of_ the moon._

_ And it seems_ like it goes on like this for-ev-

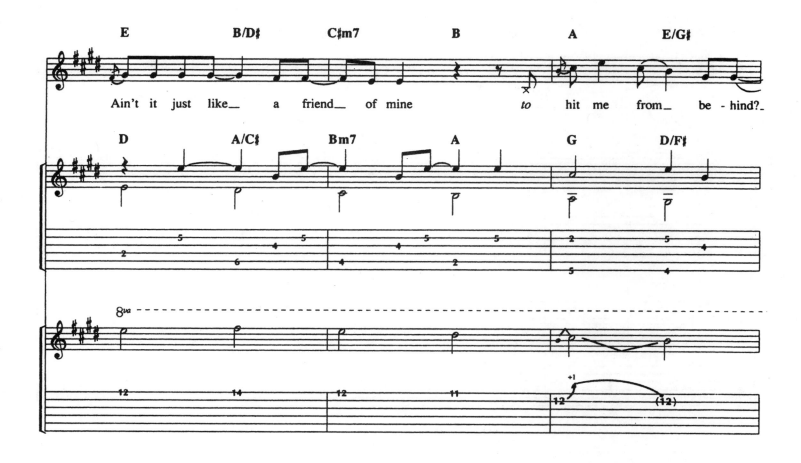

Ain't it just like___ a friend___ of mine *to* hit me from___ be - hind?___

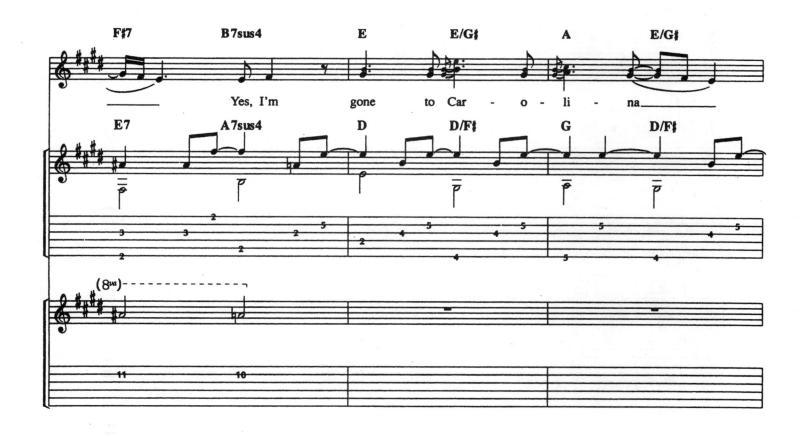

___ Yes, I'm gone to Car - o - li - na___

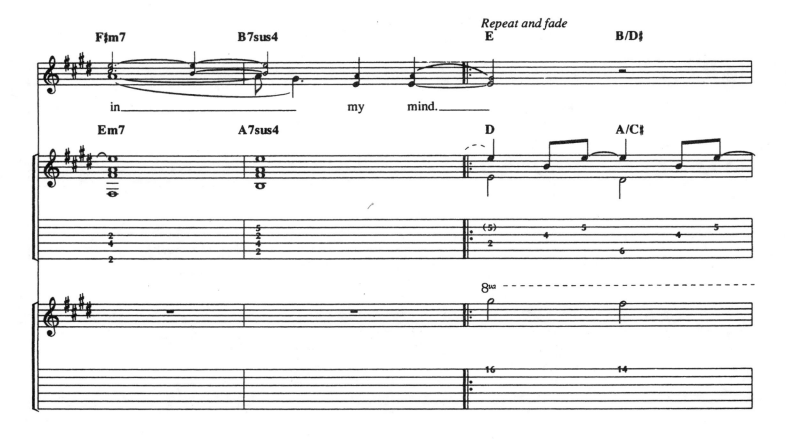

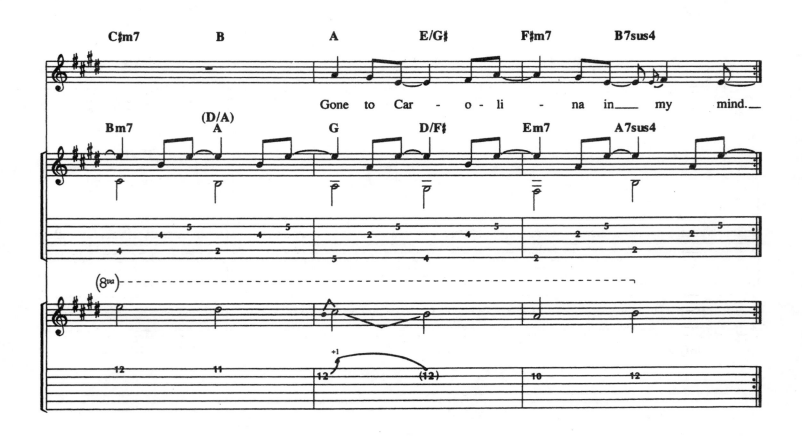

Fire and rain

Words and Music by
JAMES TAYLOR

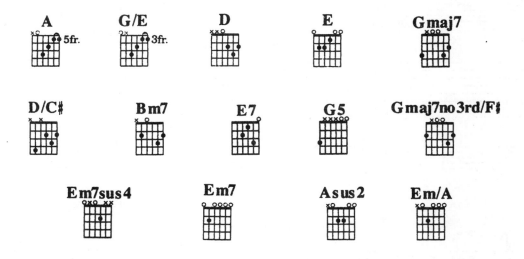

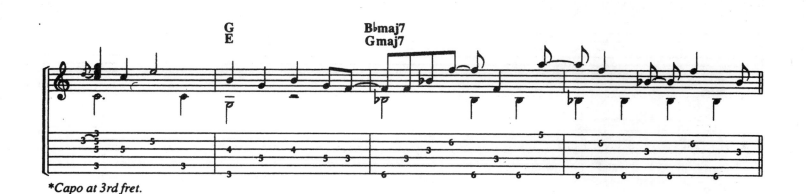

*Capo at 3rd fret.

I've seen__ lone - ly times__ when I could__

__ not__ find__ a friend.__

But I al - ways thought__ that I'd

see you__ a - gain.

With Fill 2, 2nd time.

mp

Fill 2
Guitar

Guitar maintains "Asus2" until fade. (Without capo Csus2)

Sweet baby james

Words and Music by
JAMES TAYLOR

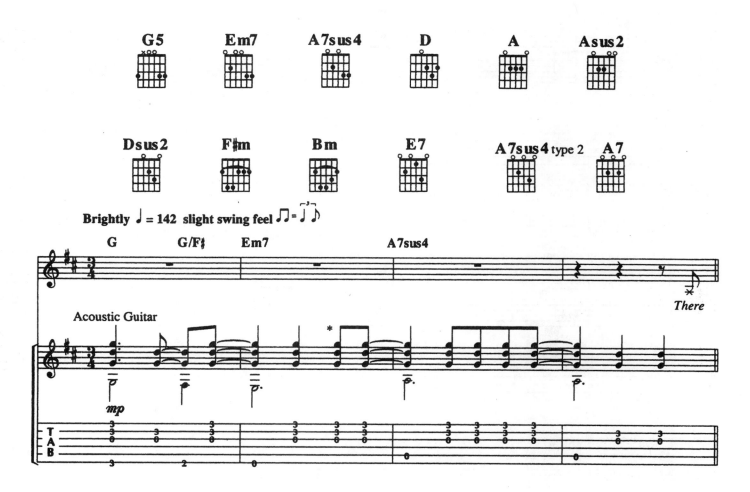

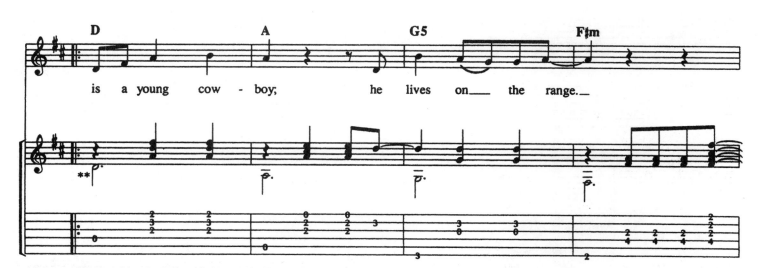

*8th note rhythms can be strummed with fingers or thumb.
**2nd Verse – ad lib. on 1st Verse line.

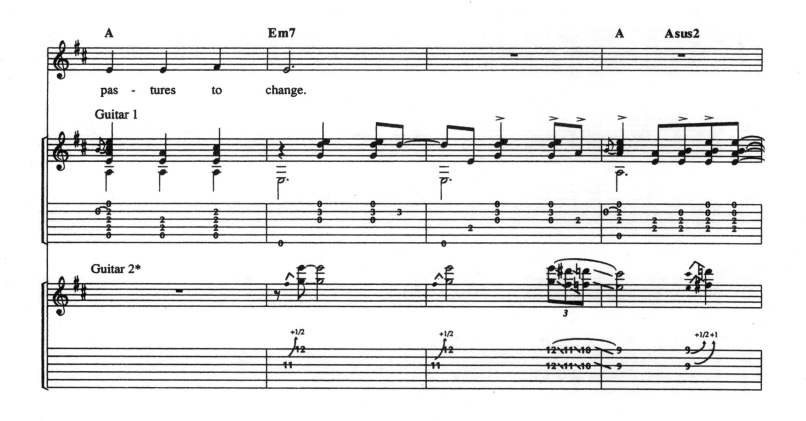

pas - tures   to   change.

And   as   the moon   ris - es   he   sits   by   his   fire,—

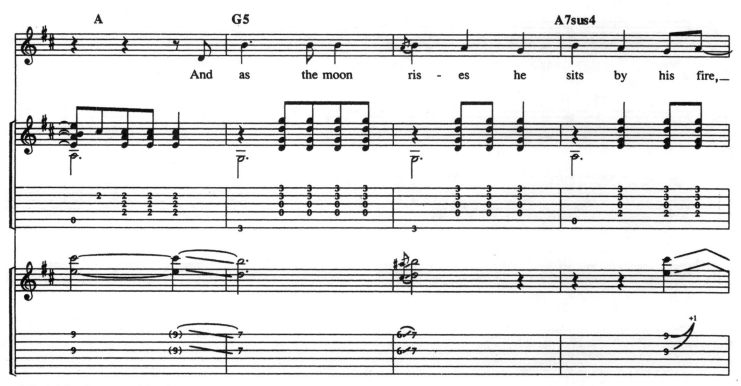

Pedal Steel arranged for Guitar.

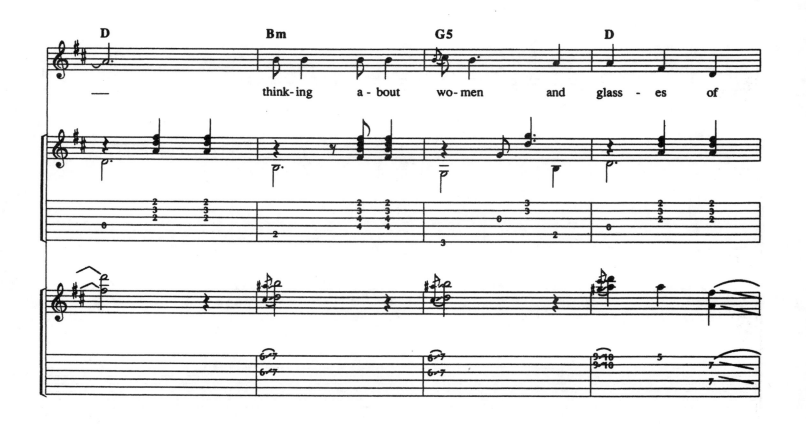

think-ing   a - bout   wo - men   and   glass - es   of

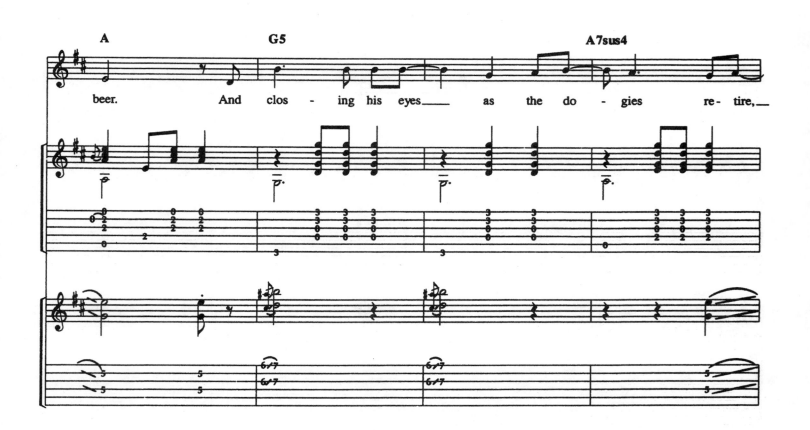

beer.   And   clos - ing his eyes___   as   the   do - gies   re - tire,___

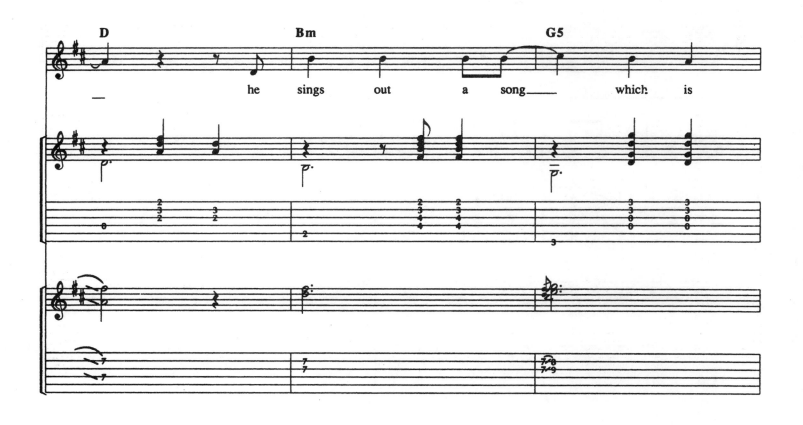

he   sings   out   a   song___   which   is

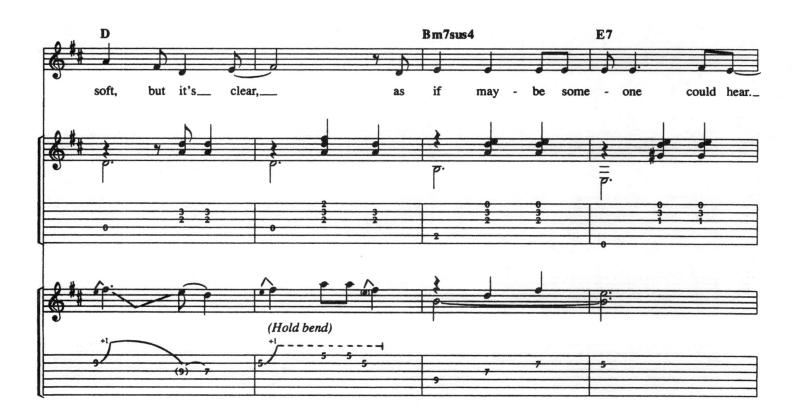

soft,   but   it's___   clear,___   as   if   may - be   some - one   could hear.___

(Hold bend)

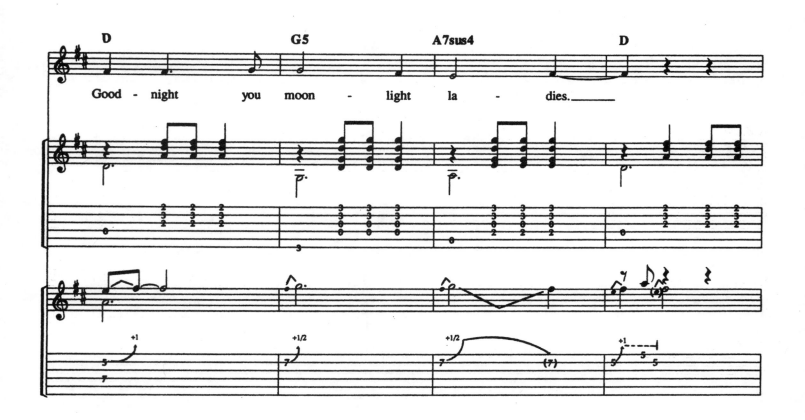

Good - night you moon - light la - dies._____

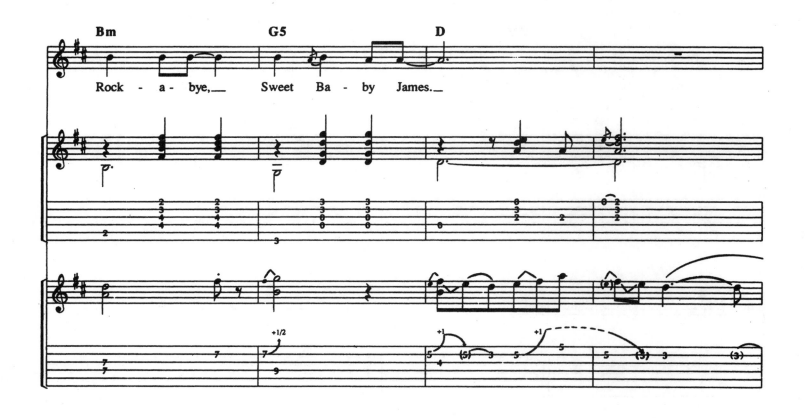

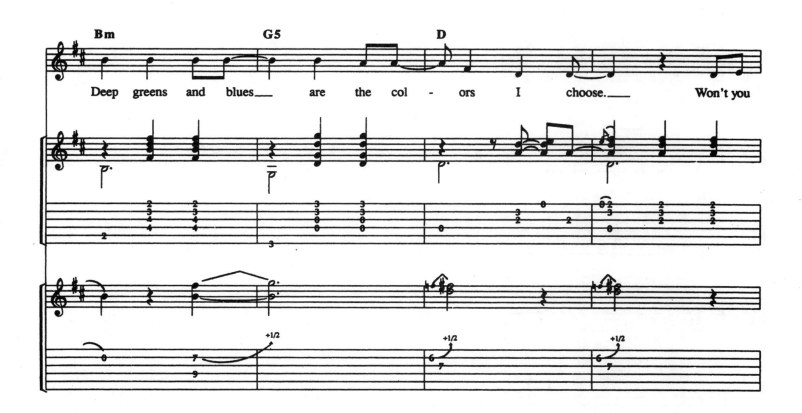

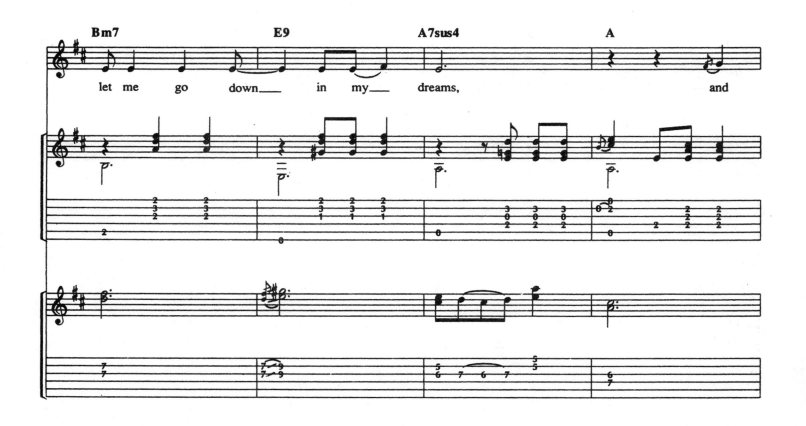

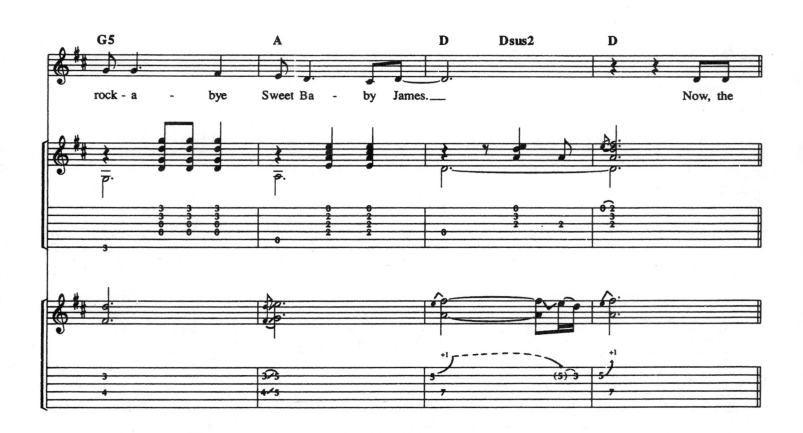

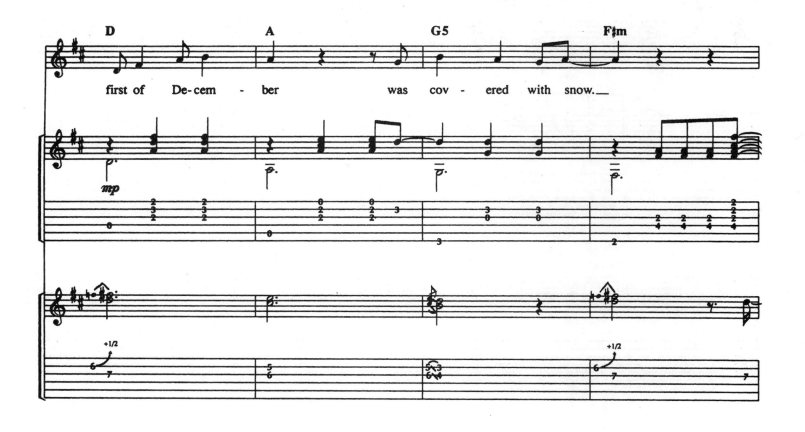

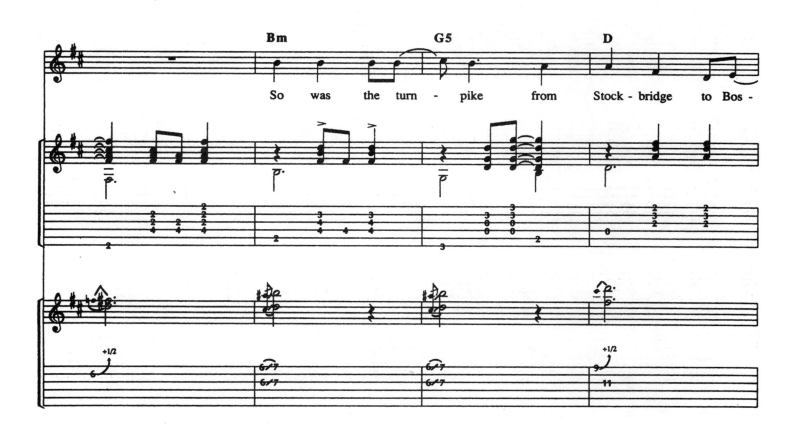

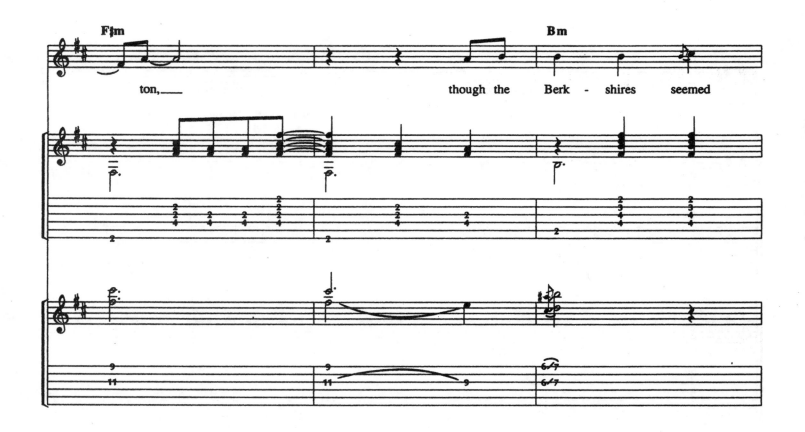

ton,___ though the Berk - shires seemed

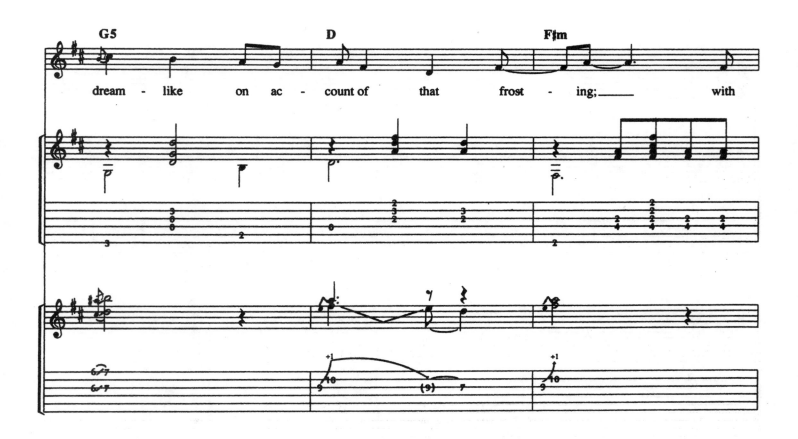

dream - like on ac - count of that frost - ing;___ with

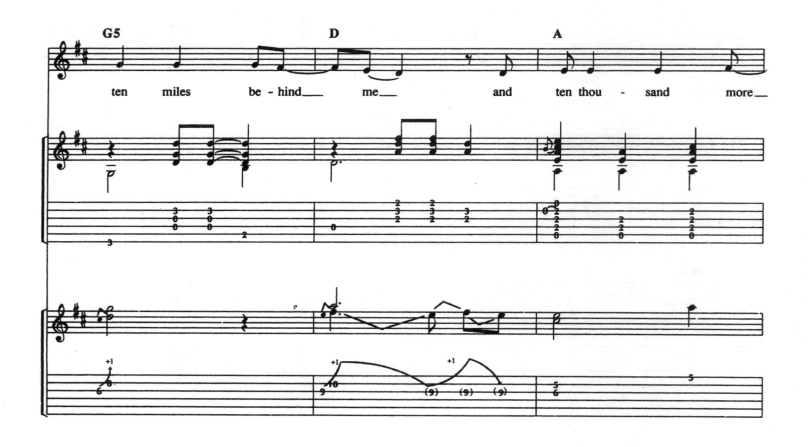

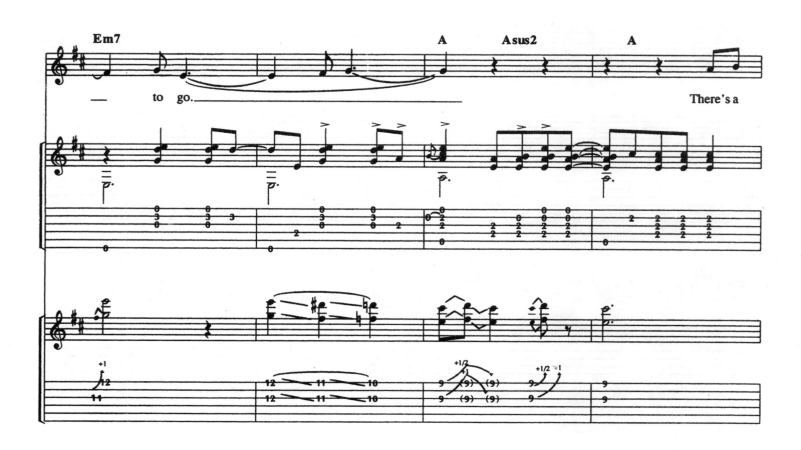

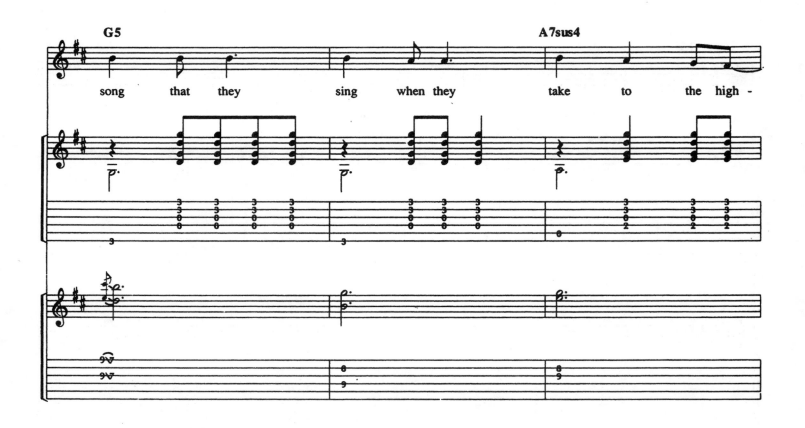

song that they sing when they take to the high -

way; a song that they sing when they take to the sea;

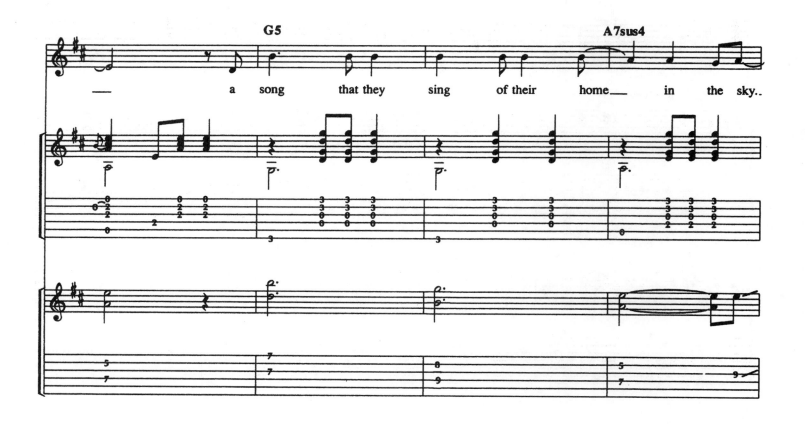

a song   that they   sing   of their   home___   in the   sky..

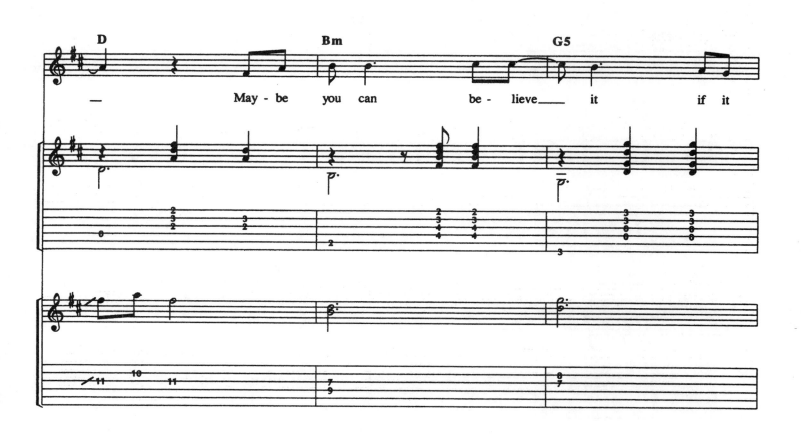

May - be   you   can   be - lieve___   it   if   it

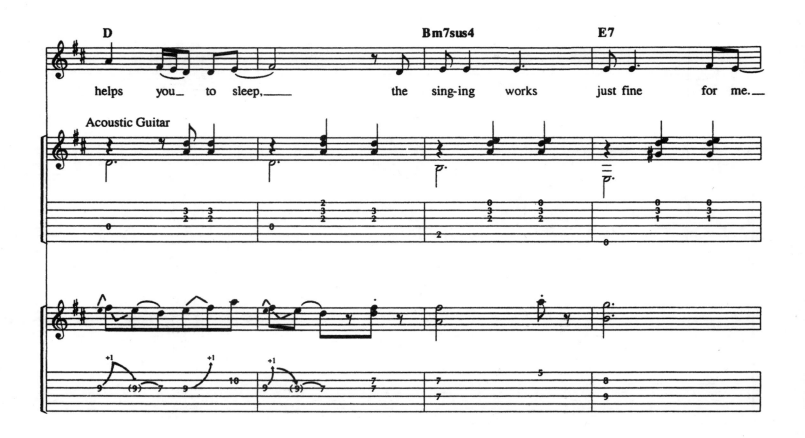

D   Bm7sus4   E7

helps   you_   to   sleep,____   the   sing-ing   works   just fine   for   me.__

Acoustic Guitar

A7sus4 Type 2

So__

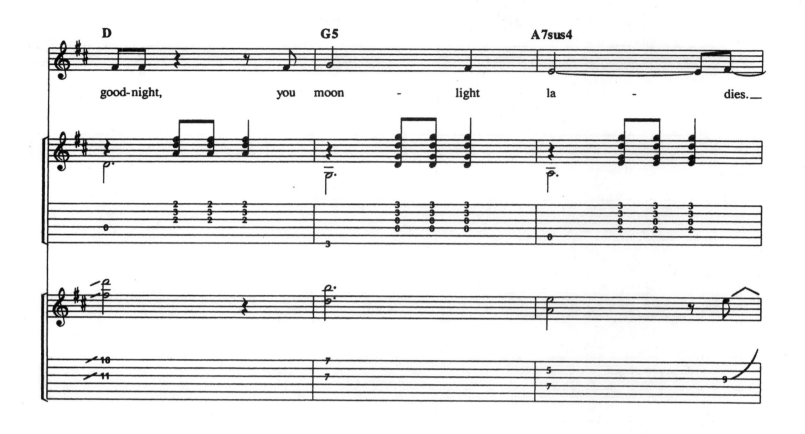

good-night, you moon - light la - dies.

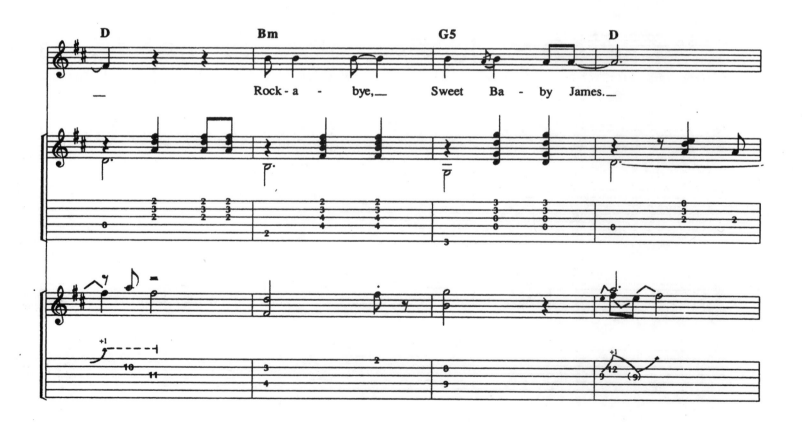

Rock - a - bye,__ Sweet Ba - by James.__

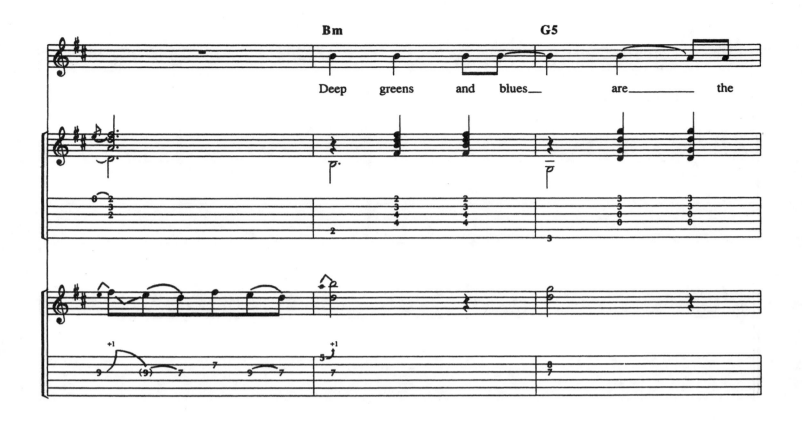

Deep   greens   and   blues___   are___   the

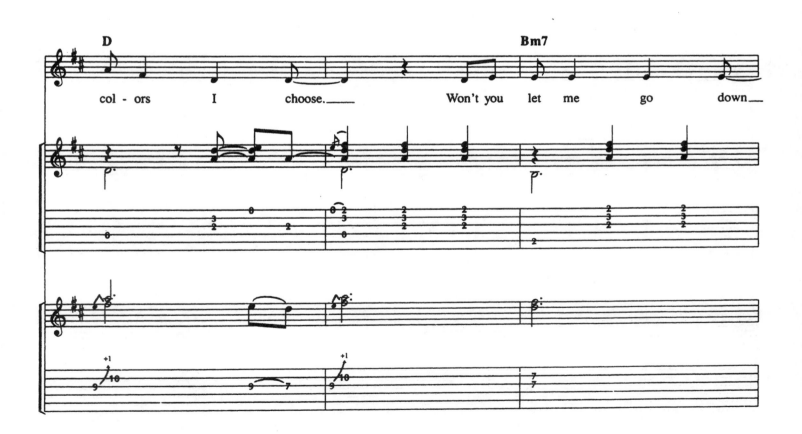

col - ors   I   choose.___   Won't you   let   me   go   down___

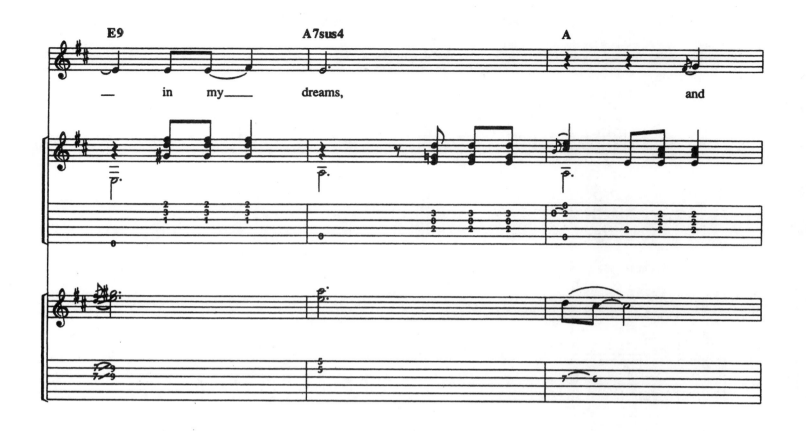

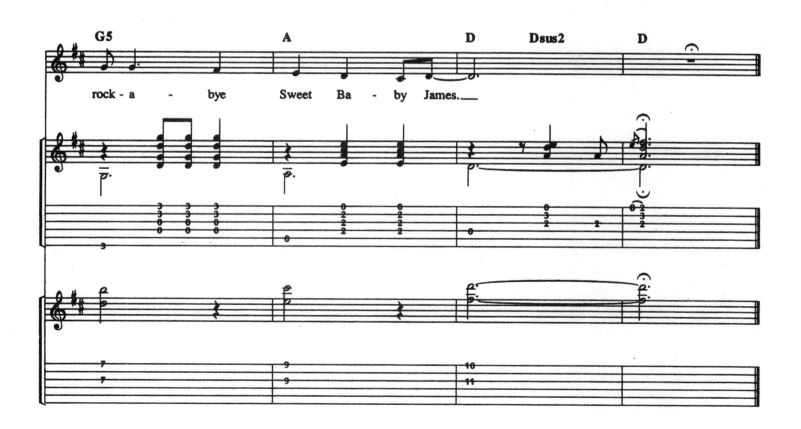

Country road

Words and Music by
JAMES TAYLOR

*Tune 6 string to D

You've got a friend

Words and Music by
CAROLE KING

*Capo on 2nd fret.

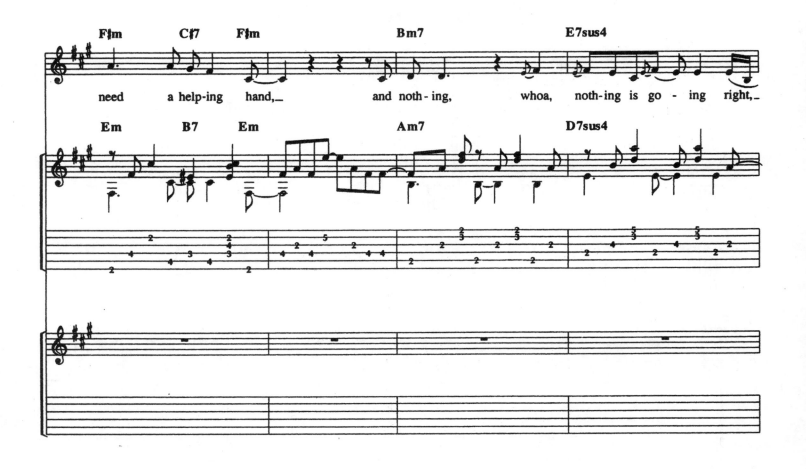

need a help-ing hand,___ and noth-ing, whoa, noth-ing is go-ing right,___

___ close you're eyes___ and think of me and

soon I will be there to bright - en up

ev - en you're dark - est night. You just call

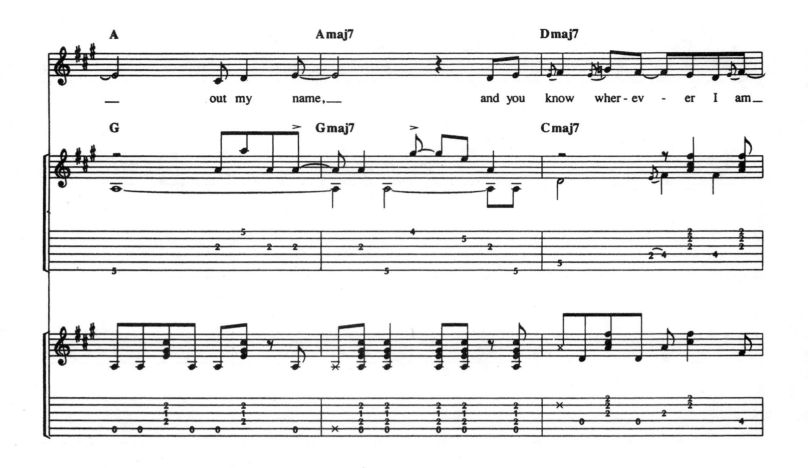

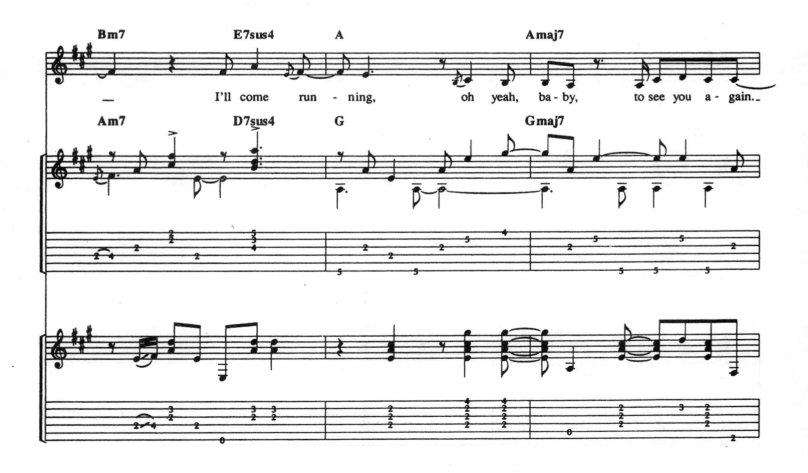

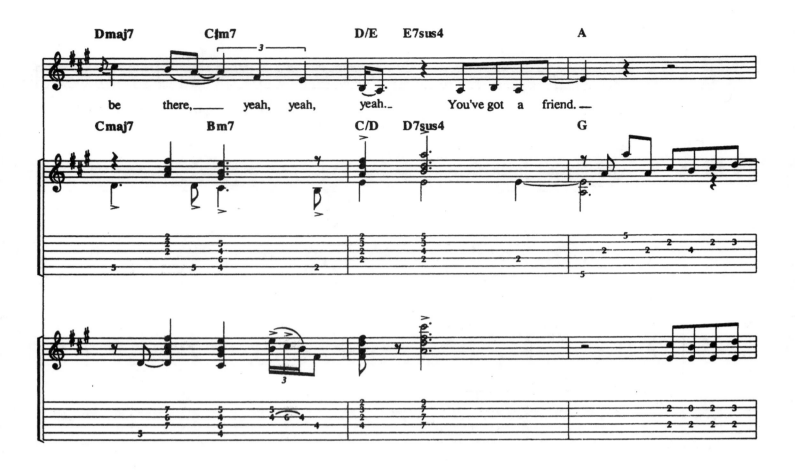

be there,____ yeah, yeah, yeah.__ You've got a friend. __

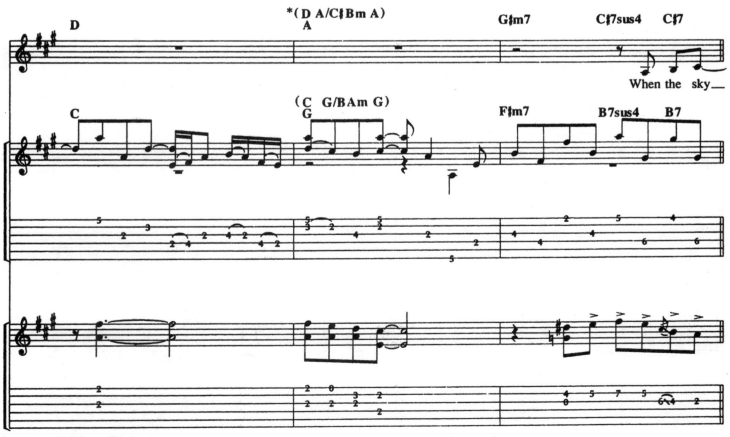

When the sky __

Harmony implied by Bass.

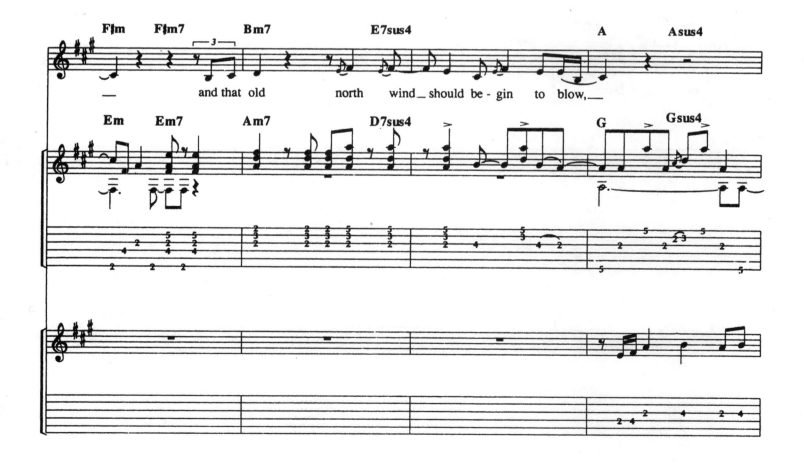

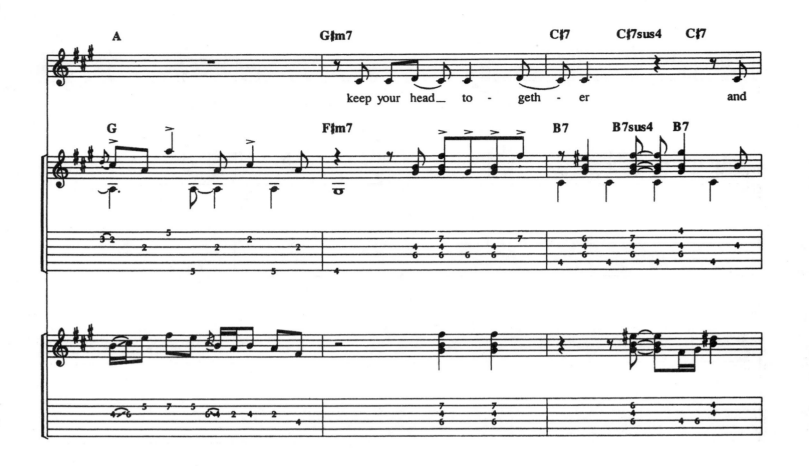

keep your head_ to - geth - er   and

call   my   name_____ out_   loud,_____ now.   Soon I'll be knock-

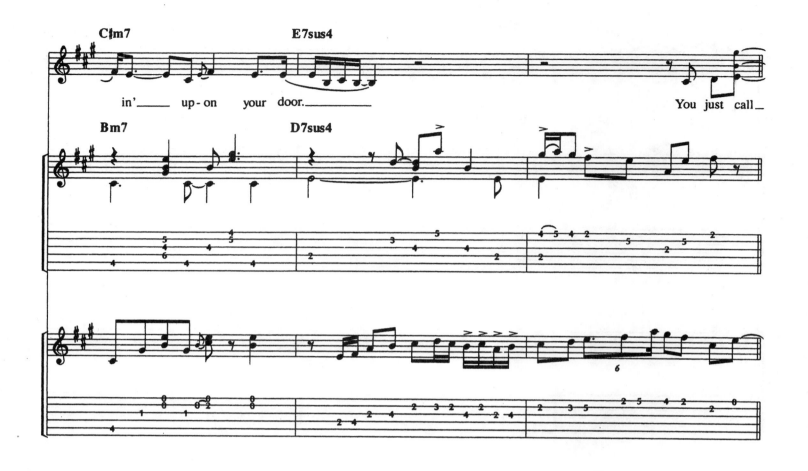

in'_____ up-on your door._____   You just call_

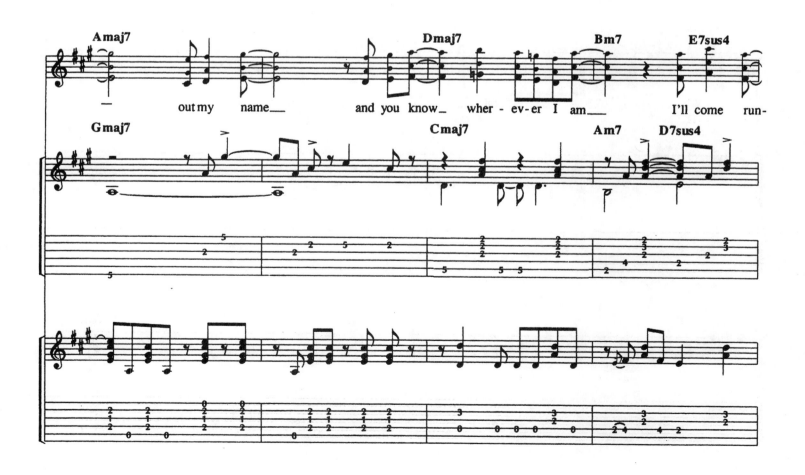

_____ out my name____ and you know_ wher-ev-er I am____ I'll come run-

ing,___ oh yes, I will, *to* see you a-gain.___

Win-ter, spring, sum-mer, or fall,_____ *yeah,* all you got to do is___ call,___

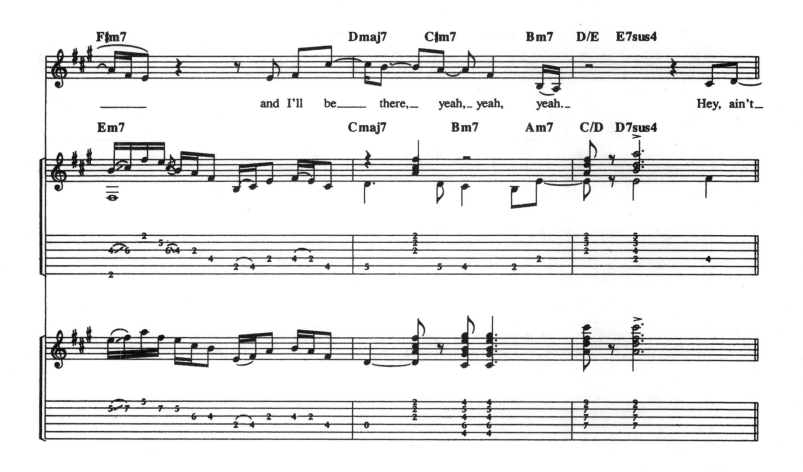

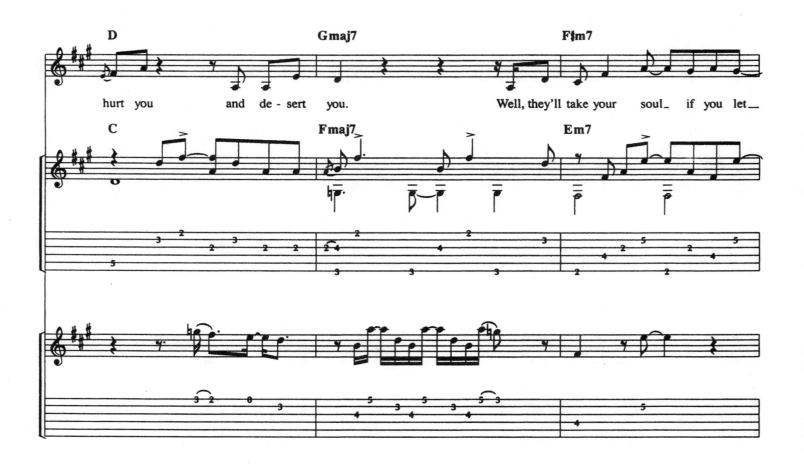

hurt you and de - sert you. Well, they'll take your soul_ if you let_

_ them. Oh, yeah, but don't_ you let them. You just call_ out my name,.

Let ring

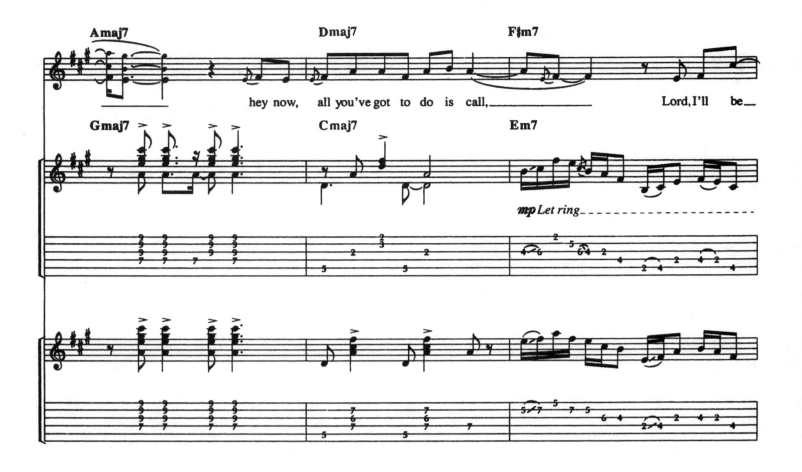

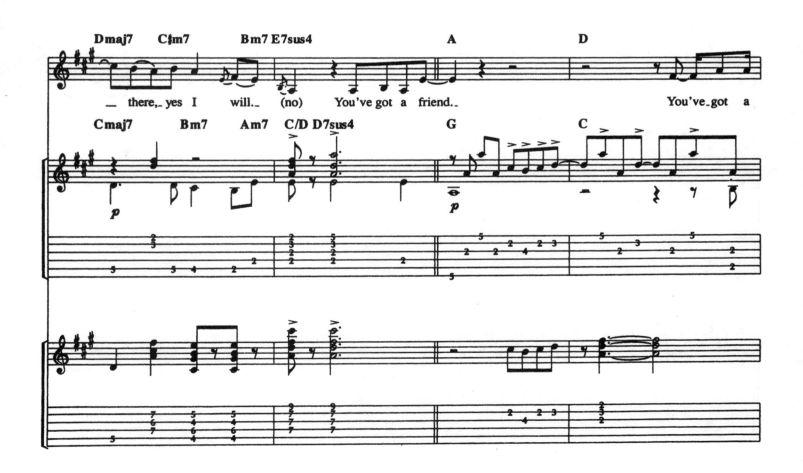

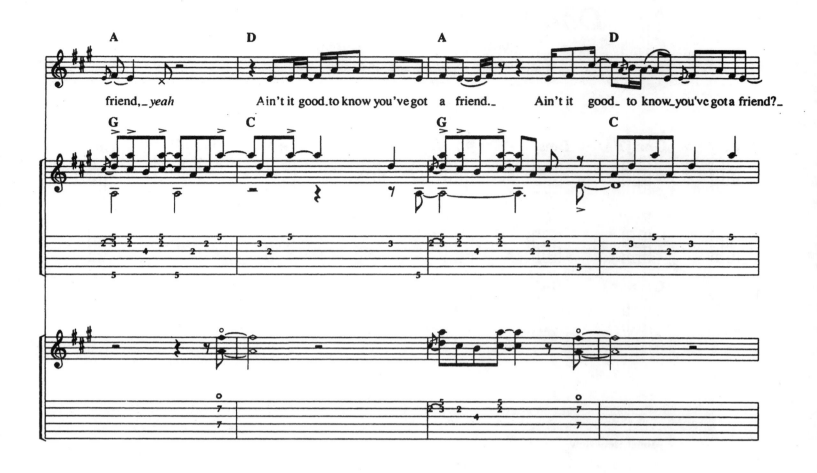

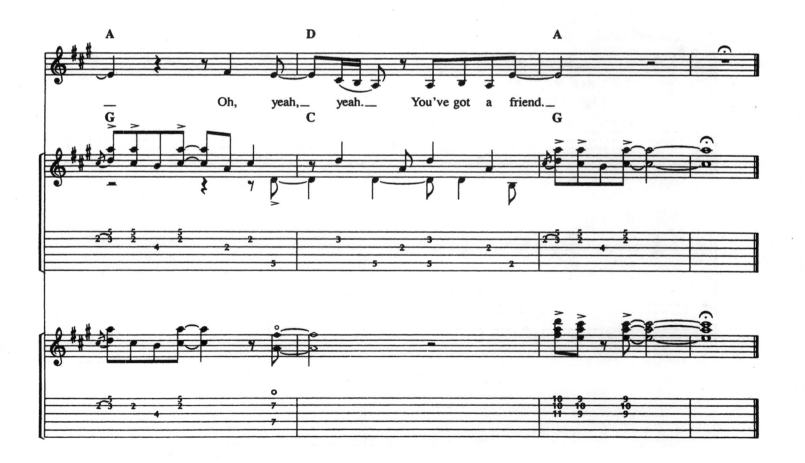

Don't let me be lonely tonight

Words and Music by
JAMES TAYLOR

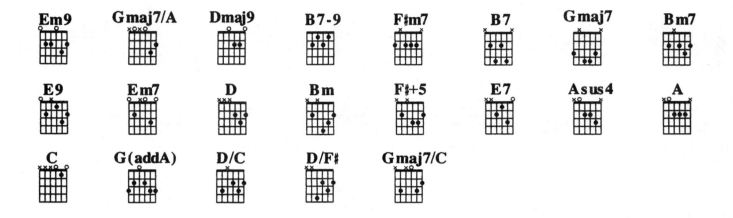

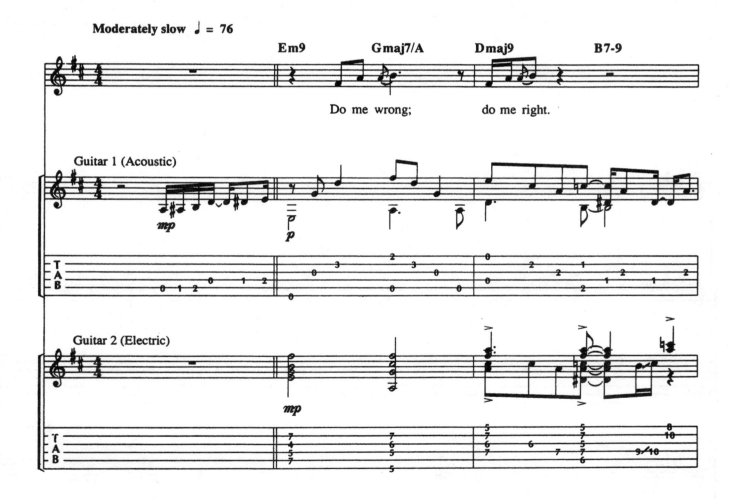

Tell me lies,— but hold— me tight.— Save your good-byes for— the morn-

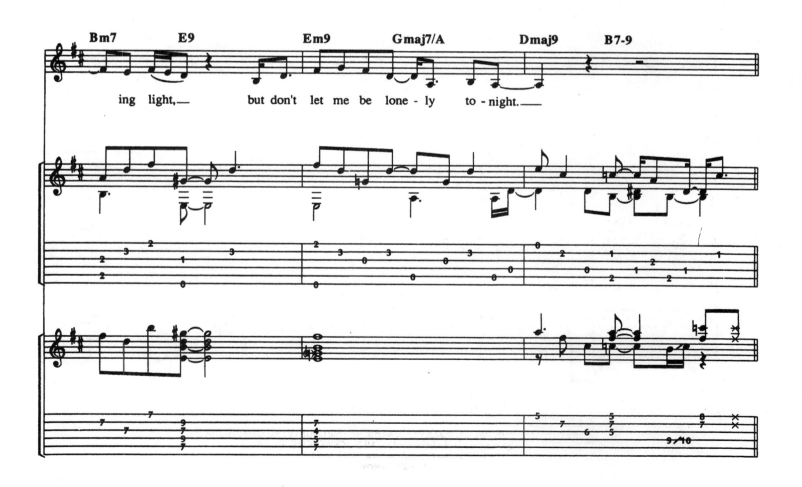

ing light,— but don't let me be lone - ly to - night.—

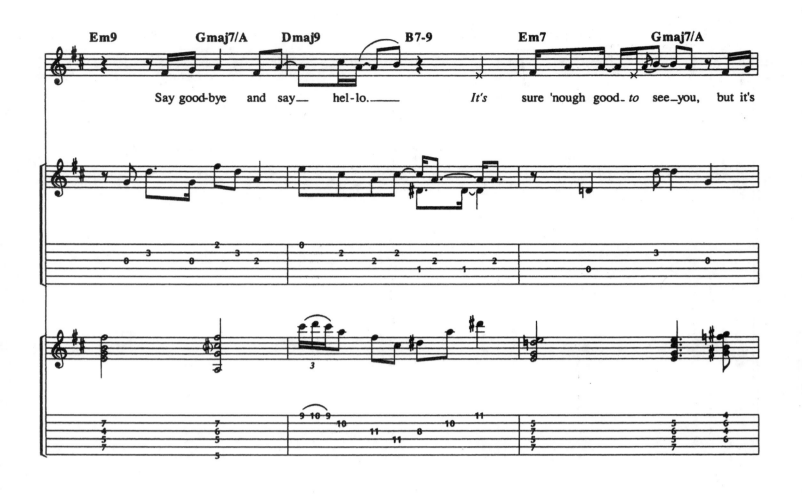

Say good-bye and say_ hel-lo.___ *It's* sure 'nough good_ *to* see_you, but it's

time to go.___ Don't say yes but_ please don't say__ no.__ I don't

I'm un-de-cid-ed   and your heart's been di-vid-ed.   You've been   turn-ing   my   world   up-side

down,   no,   no.   *So*   do me   wrong;

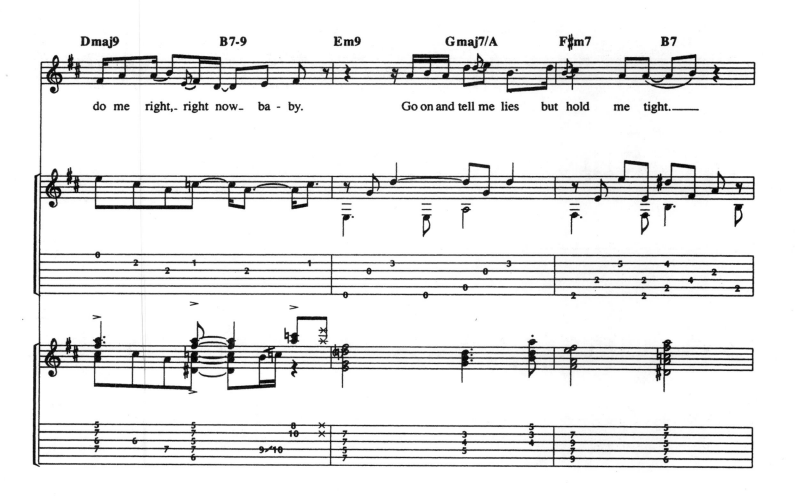

do me right,- right now— ba - by. Go on and tell me lies but hold me tight.____

Save your good-byes for the morn - in' light morn-in' light,— but don't let me be lone-ly to-night.

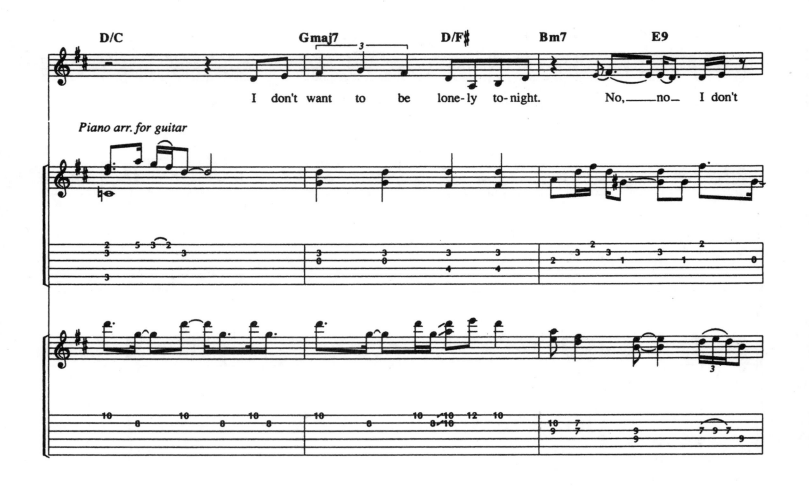

Piano arr. for guitar

I don't want to be lone-ly to-night. No,——no— I don't

want to— be lone-ly to-night.—

Walking man

Words and Music by
JAMES TAYLOR

Moderately slow, in 2 ♩ = 76

Intro:

Guitar 1 (Acoustic)

Guitar 2 (Electric)

Mov-ing in

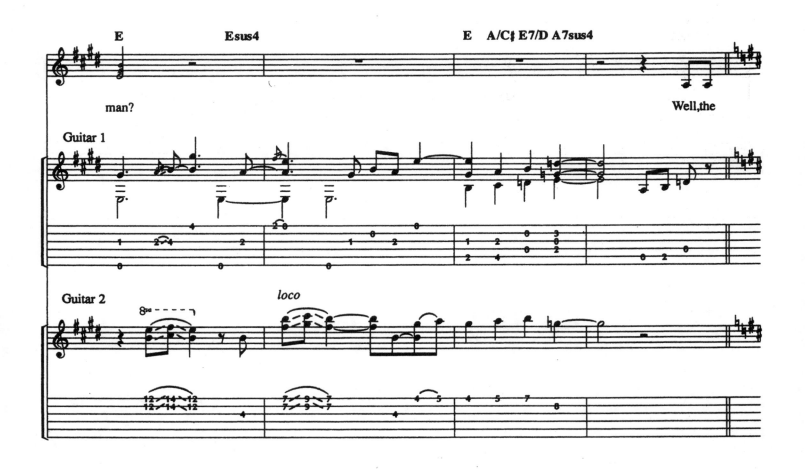

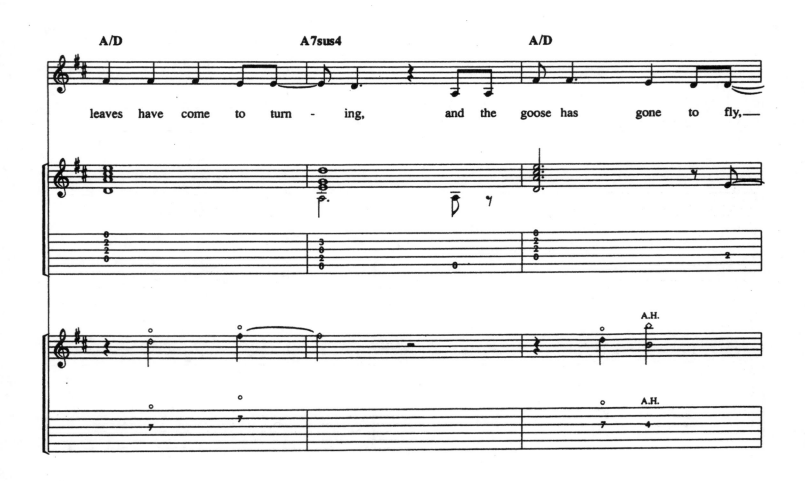

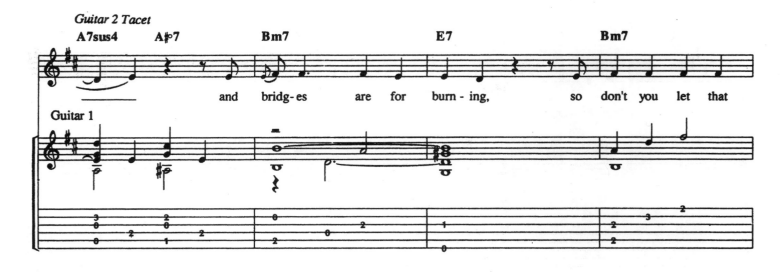

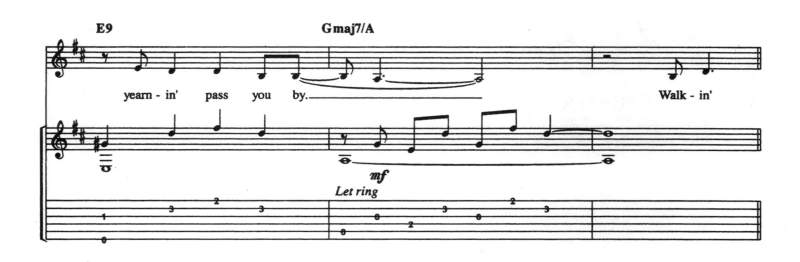

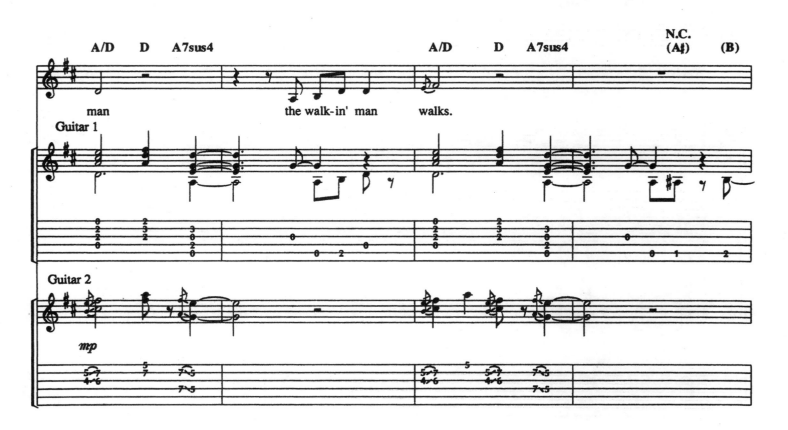

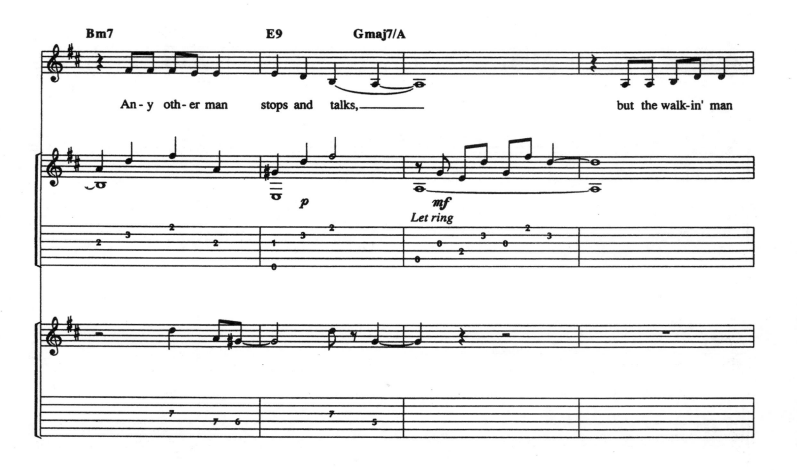

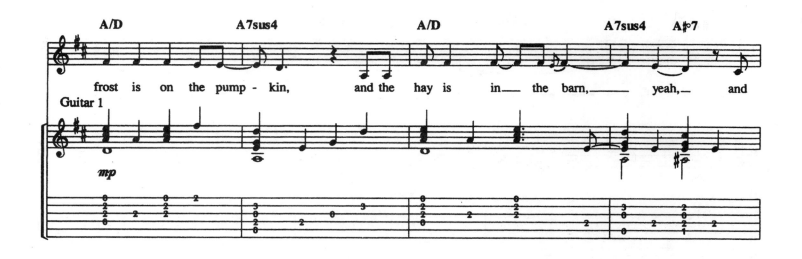

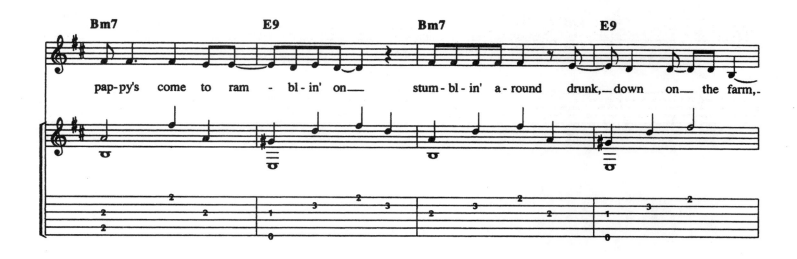

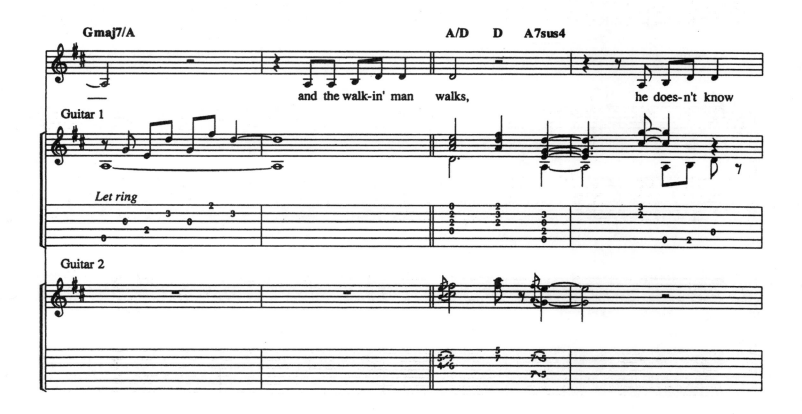

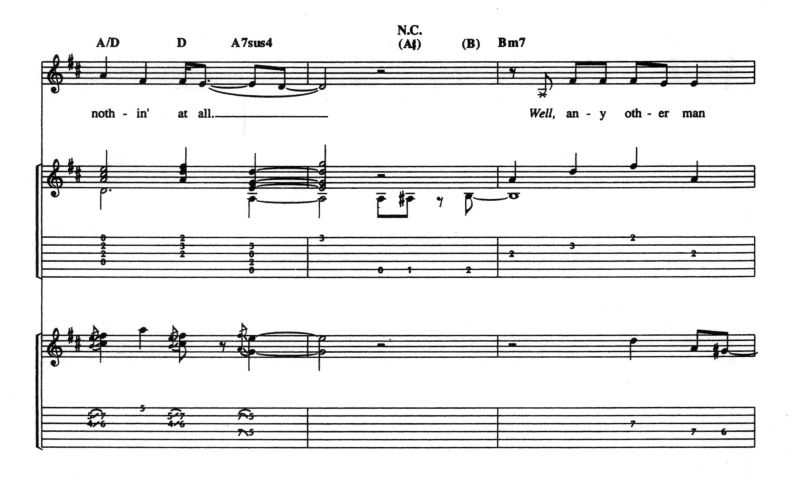

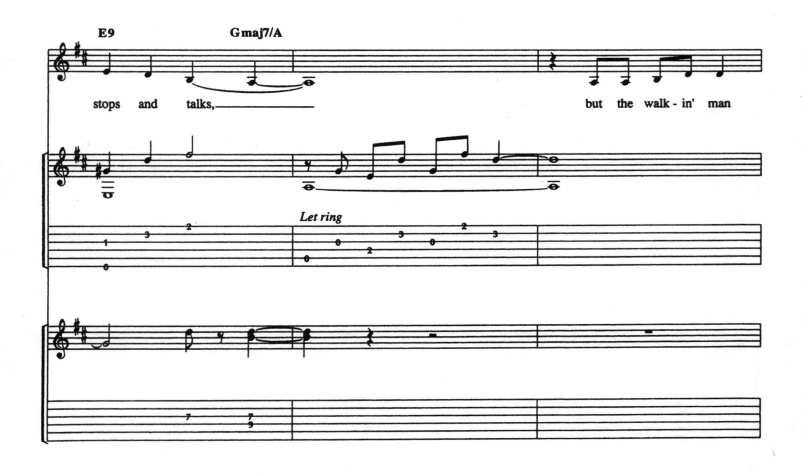

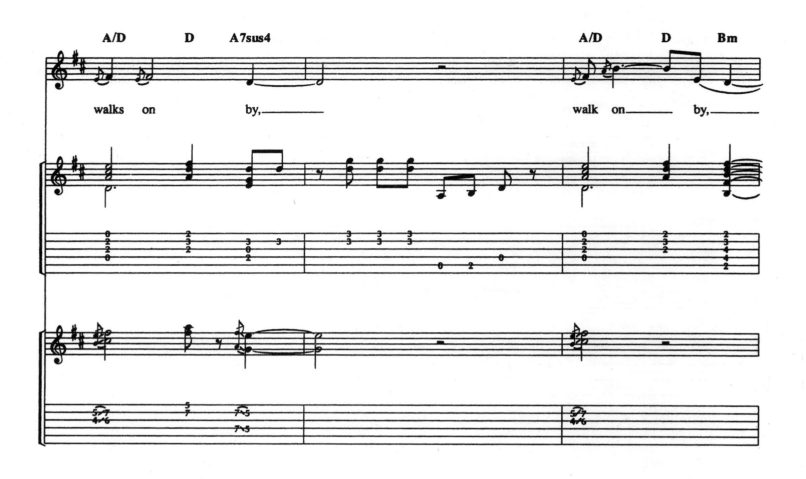

walks on by,_____ walk on____ by,_____

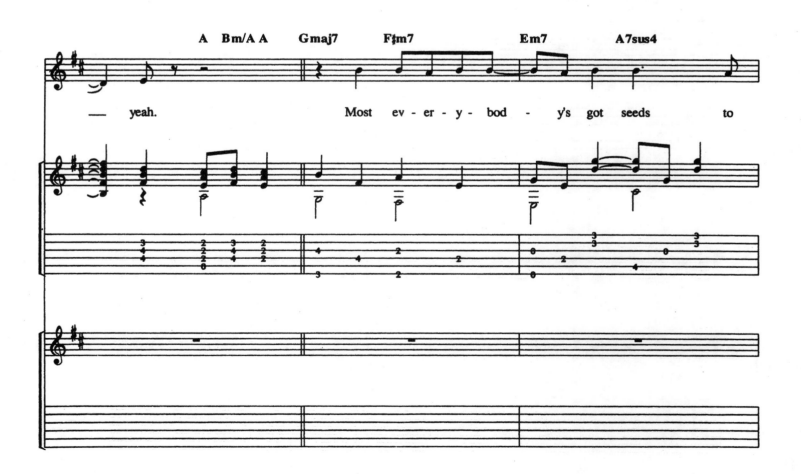

— yeah. Most ev - er - y - bod - y's got seeds to

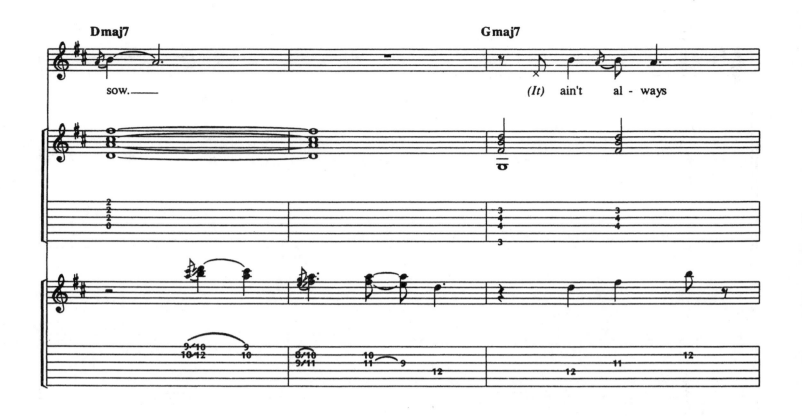

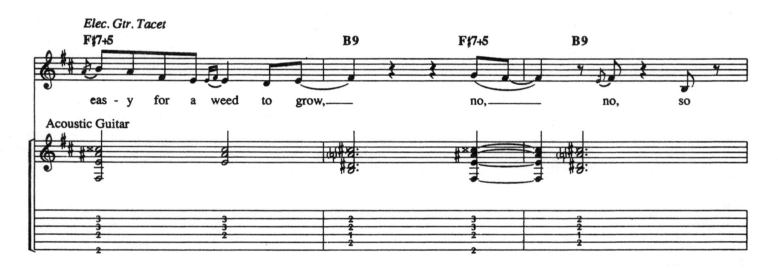

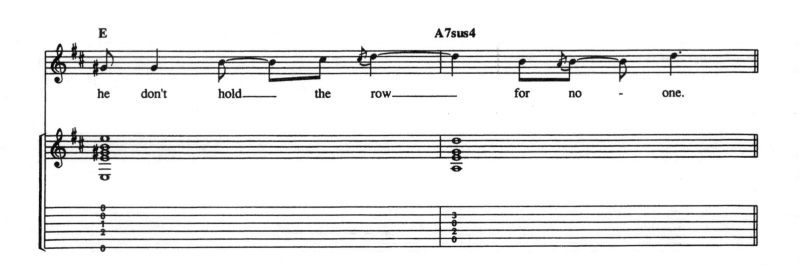

*Acoustic Guitar overdub.

How sweet it is (to be loved by you)

Words and Music by
EDDIE HOLLAND,
LAMONT DOZIER and BRIAN HOLLAND

*Piano arranged for Guitar.

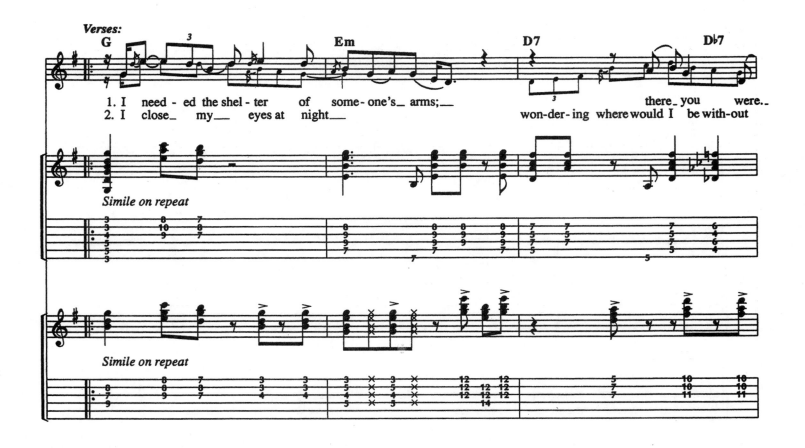

Verses:

1. I need-ed the shel-ter of some-one's arms;___ there you were..
2. I close my eyes at night___ won-der-ing where would I be with-out

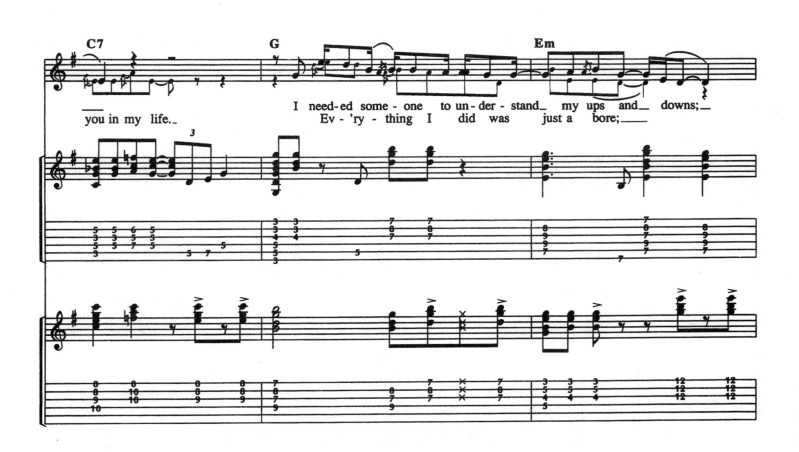

you in my life..___ I need-ed some-one to un-der-stand my ups and downs;___
Ev-'ry-thing I did was just a bore;___

ev - 'ry-where I went seems I'd been there be - fore. But

With Fill 1 on D.S.

With_ sweet_ love an' de - vo-tion_ deep - ly touch - ing my_ e - mo-
you bright - en up for me all_ of my days_ with a_ love so sweet in
See additional lyrics

Fill 1
Guitar 3 *loco*

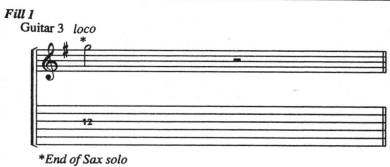

End of Sax solo

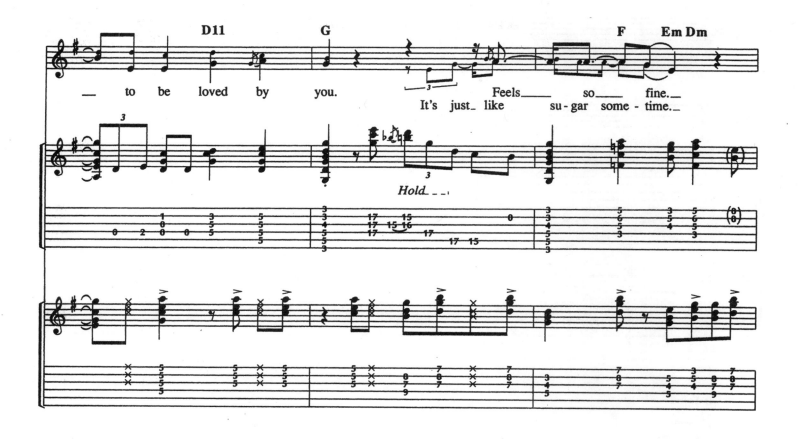

*Sax arranged for Guitar.

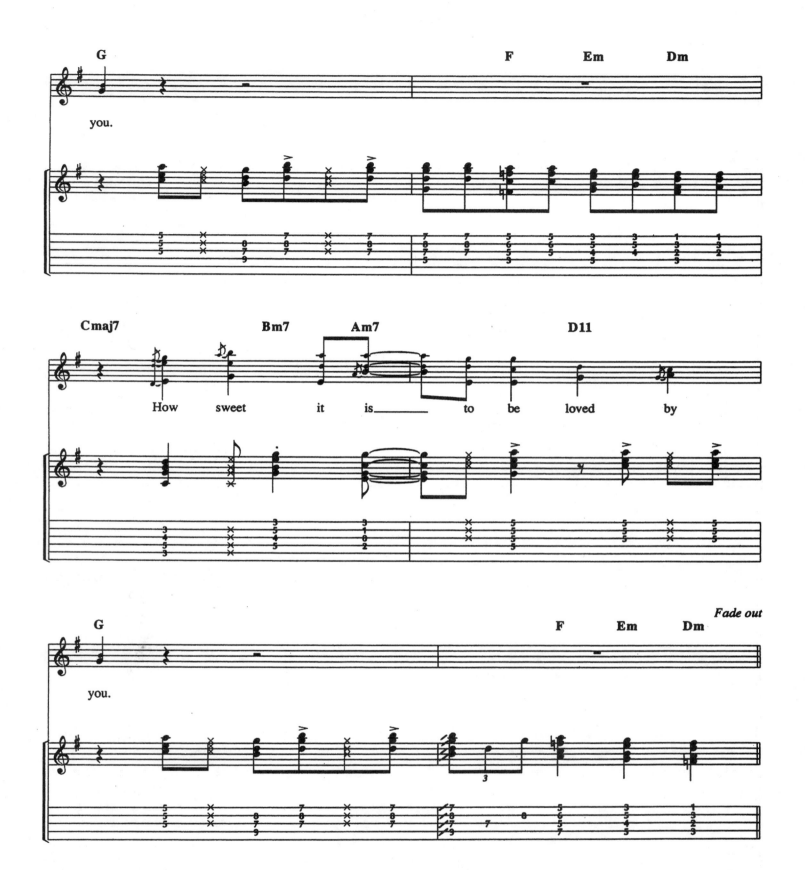

Additional Lyrics

You were better to me than I was to myself;
For me there's you and there ain't nobody else.
I want to . . .

Mexico

Words and Music by
JAMES TAYLOR

*Capo at 2nd fret. Two acoustic guitars arranged as one.

Shower the people

Words and Music by
JAMES TAYLOR

You can play the game and you can act out the part, though you

know it was-n't writ-ten for you. *But* tell me how you can stand there with your

*Capo at 3rd fret.

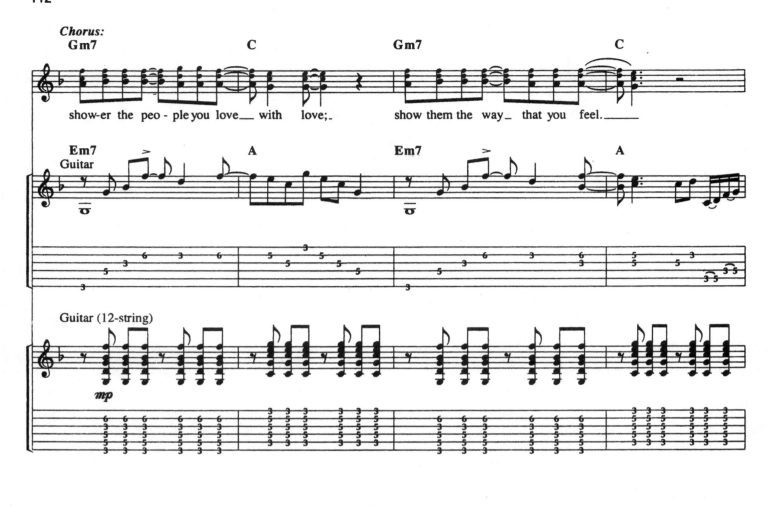

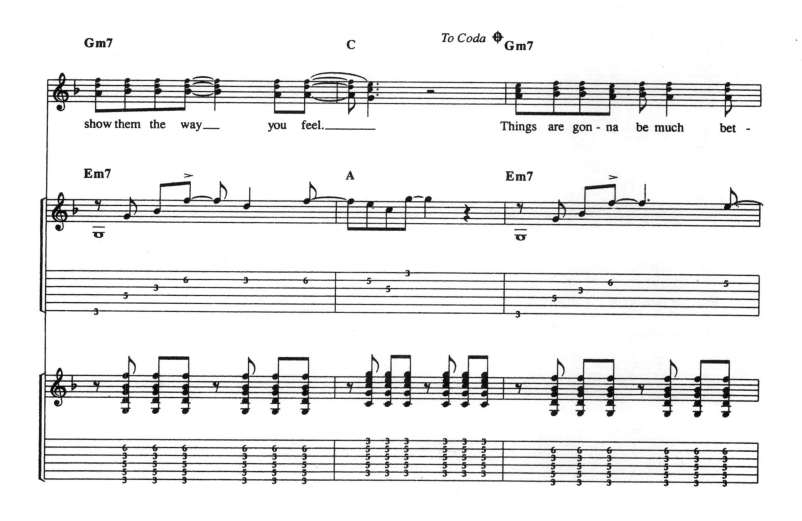

114

Played by Bass.

⊕ *Coda*

Things are gon-na be much bet-ter if you on-ly will.____

Whoa,____

Repeat and fade

Show-er the peo-ple you love_ with love;____ show them the way_ that you feel.____

_ *(Ad lib. Vocal)*___

Additional Lyrics

Ad lib. Vocal: They say in every life,
They say the rain must fall.
Just like the pouring rain,
Make it rain.

Love is sunshine.
Love, love love is sunshine.
Make it rain
Love, love love is sunshine. Alright, yeah.
Everybody, everybody, everybody, everybody.

Steamroller

Words and Music by
JAMES TAYLOR

*Capo at 3rd fret. The number 3 in tab represents a capoed open string.

Yeah, I'm a ce - ment mix - er for_ you, ba - by, yeah, ha; a churn-

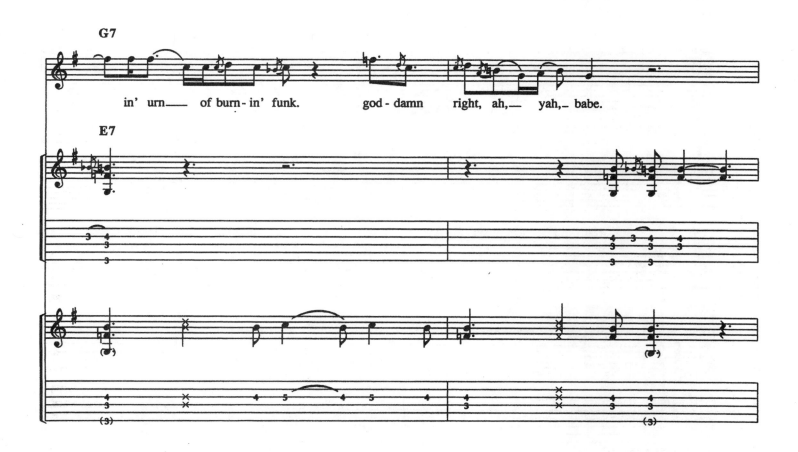

in' urn____ of burn - in' funk. god - damn right, ah,____ yah,_ babe.

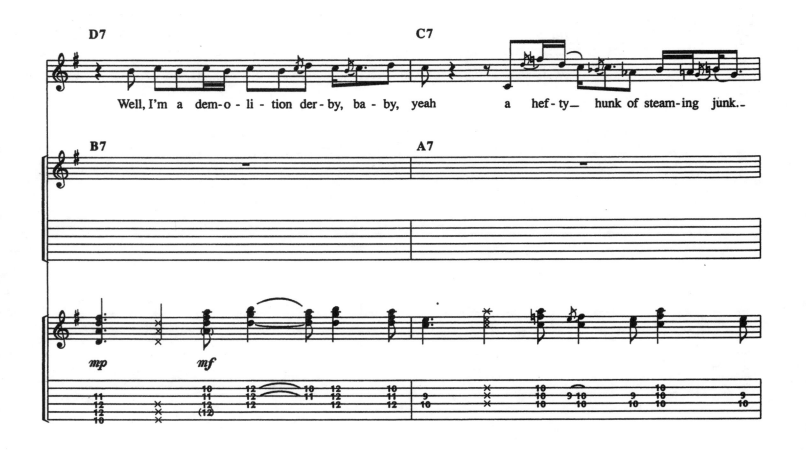

Well, I'm a dem-o - li - tion der - by, ba - by, yeah   a   hef - ty hunk of steam-ing junk.

Mis - ter Mac D. got the blues for you an' me.   Fly a - way to say "nah, babe."

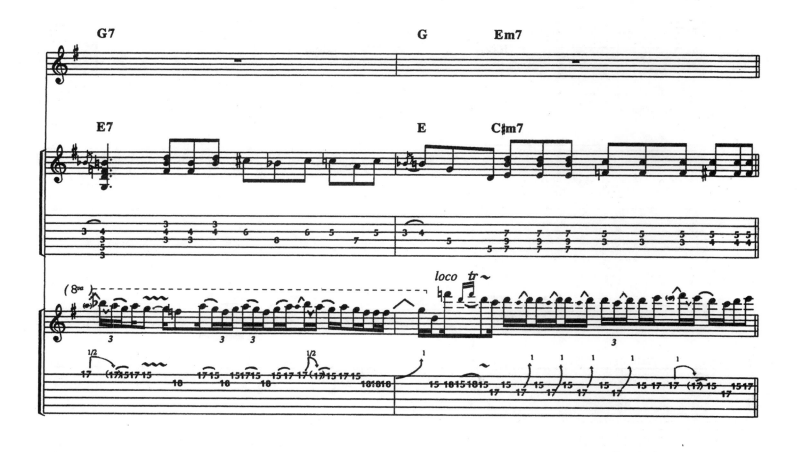

Well, I'm a na - palm bomb for you, ba - by.

Stone—

G7

guar-an-teed— to blow your mind— high - er.

Drop a

E7

cresc. poco a poco

C7

na - palm bomb for you, babe, got to tell ya one more time. to sit   down,   stand up, go home;—   back to L. A.—

A7

mp

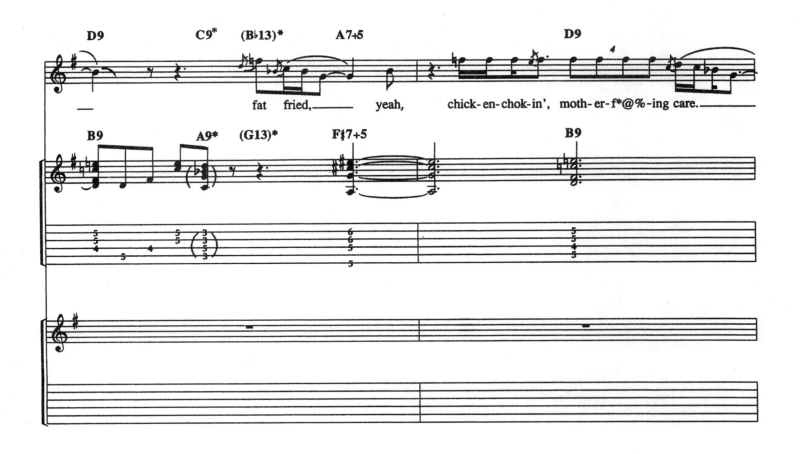

fat fried,_____ yeah, chick-en-chok-in', moth-er-f*@%-ing care._____

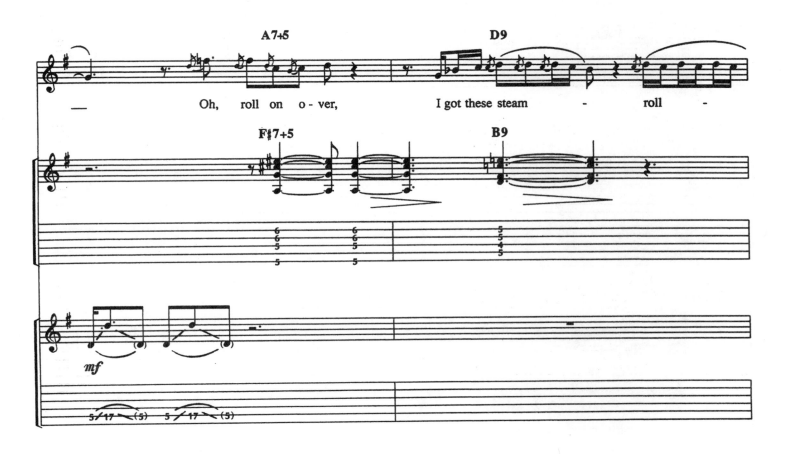

Oh, roll on o - ver, I got these steam - roll -

*Piano

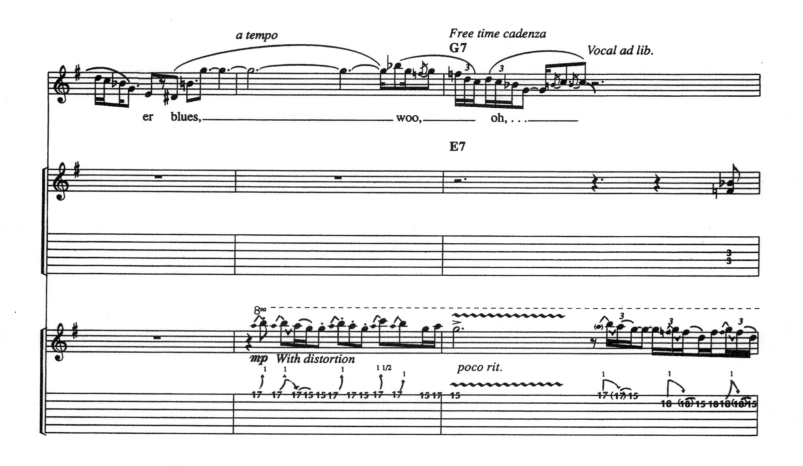

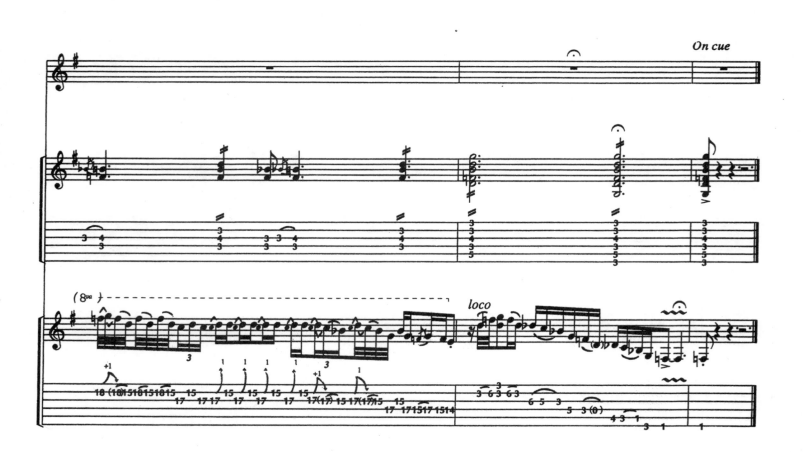